THE

ESCAPE

PLAN

Published in the United States of America

First Printing Edition, 2026

ISBN 0-0000000-0-0

MEN DONT GIVE UP

There Still Great Women Out Here To Get Married To

You Can Still Live A Successful Life And Escape A Toxic Woman Or Man

PAY LITTLE CHILD SUPPORT AND NO ALIMONY

THE

ESCAPE

PLAN

CHECKMATE

Yup, this book gonna be all types of wrong gramma,,..... but all true stories... The **Escape Plan** will contain grammatical errors such as, incorrect spacing, misspelled words, uncapitalized words, incorrect grammar and punctuation. My honeydew wanted it this way. Everything doesn't have to be perfect, if it gets the job done and message out. Some things are best in there rawest form. Keep it simple smarty............K.I.S.S.

Table of Contents

Thank you, God

Thank you to Lady E, three baby daddies. Thank you for doing what you did, when you did it, how you did it, why you did it. Just thank you. My life is calm, peaceful, and fulfilling with my wife, Lady E. You didn't know, you were literally standing on top of your own diamond mine. I just had to go a little further and deeper to reach a land full of riches that was always there.

So, thank you.

Thank you to Honeydews ex-wife's number one and number two. Thank you for doing everything that you did when you did it, how you did it, why you did it, just thank you. Because it led my Honeydew directly to me... my Honeydew is the best. I can't even picture my life without him. I got exactly what I was praying for when I thought all the doors had been closed for me. All I had to do was go down the hallway and there was another door that was gently cracked just waiting for the right person to step in. Let me tell you why I am so thankful to x-wife 1 and 2.

I go to sleep every night with my Honeydew smiling and he wakes me up every morning smiling, playing beautiful music and prayer. "I woke up like this". We both look out the window of my yacht. And we thank the Lord for waking us up to an endless view of water. We hit the onsite gym or go for a walk alongside the lake or river holding hands listening to music. Then honeydew makes us breakfast to eat outside on the bridge deck while we watch the sun rise. Then my honeydew makes my green tea and prepares my lunch in the kitchen of my yacht. While I get ready for work. Sometimes honeydew writes a little love you note on a Post-it and hides it in my lunch or in my SUV. And throughout the day when we talk, he asks me to find where he left the note. It's like a little treasure hunt. He already has my scrubs cleaned washed and smelling very good with fabric softener. He has my socks and all my undergarments picked out for me in the morning. My honeydew walks me down the dock to my SUV, hugs and gives me a kiss and tells me that I'm great. And I'm going to see 10 clients today, and he will be waiting for me when I get home.

And when I come home to my honeydew at night. He already has dinner prepared with my holy water. He rubs my feet because I've been on them all day. Then we cut on the tv and watch our favorite shows while Honeydew goes to my second vehicle. He cleans it out because I see 10 clients a day and I just get in the SUV and throw all the things in the back. Honeydew cleans out all the trash, reorganizes my medical bag, just like I want it, Honeydew goes and fills up my SUV with gas, gets it washed and brings it back. Honeydew comes back on the yacht and chills with me, we finish eating, watch TV and I beat him playing cards. Sometimes we go out and sit on the back of the yacht before it starts getting cold at night and we just dance. Or we might take the yacht out into the river or lake, anchor down, sit out in the water and dance under the moonlight. On the weekends, when we're here in Michigan, we might hang out with friends, club, or honeydew and I cruise in one of his family inherited classic vehicles, take the top off and go to eat where ever we want, go where ever we want and just cruise the night away… One of his family inherited vehicles has hydraulics and switches. When we do valet, we don't even do valet. Lady E pays for Honeydew to valet, just to park the 77 up front. Honeydew puts it in three-wheel motion and leaves it hanging, just sitting there till we come out of wherever we go. He laughs and smiles while we are in the restaurant. Saying **"Thank you God"**. Of all his family inherited vehicles, I believe the 77 is Honeydew's favorite. Even though Honeydew loves the beast. I think he likes the 77 the most. He makes this face when he's hitting them switches while riding down a crowded street. Honeydew little face is so adorable when he hits the switches. Then we wake up the next morning and do the same thing all over again to accomplish our goals. Or get ready to hop on a flight to go travel in the US or out of the country.

And when we're in Michigan to work my minimum mandatory three shifts of 12 hours(36 Hours). Which I do consecutively, starting Friday, Saturday and Sunday once a month at the hospital. Honeydew comes every day and brings me lunch. And we sit and eat together, and laugh, and joke and watch funny videos on his laptop.

Honeydew is such a great Dad to our daughter, he, helps her, with her homework, celebrates with her when she gets all A's, on her report card, attends PTA meetings with me, attends pick up and drop off at school, goes to Birthday parties, they wrench on the 77 together, a currently teaching her to drive so he can give her one of his extra vehicles to be more independent.

So thank you.

Checkmate

Chapter 1

First Conversation

Do you still Wanna Stick Around, Sign a Pre-nup and Post-nup?

I saw my Honeydew on a social media dating site November 2024. I loved all of his photos. One was a picture of him deep, underwater smiling with just some swim trunks on. I liked this photo and commented and said "you have a very nice smile". Yes, I, Lady E, reached out first to my soon to be husband Honeydew.

It took him a couple days to message back. But he said thank you for commenting on his photo he also commented on one of my photos. It was a photo of me and in a swimsuit. His comment was I see there was a cheetah loose in Michigan, I guess you caught it. Do you still have enough of that cheetah left to make me a belt. LOL…. A brother needs to coordinate..

Honeydew made me laugh. I went on to read his social media dating bio. I wanted to see what type of work he did. His work bio stated "he made sweaters for mice. LOL"…..

He made me laugh without him even being around.

I messaged him back and said… where were you at in the photo where you were underwater smiling?

Honeydew messaged me back and said that he was free diving in the Dominican Republic.. He said that he loved to travel and his goal, in life was to travel once a month and see the world. He ask me where had I traveled too?

I responded back about six places that I have been. He responded back with a laundry list of all the places that he had traveled to. Most of the places he listed where out of the country, some of the places were in the United States. And he even said that he didn't want to list all the places that he had been in the United States because he travels so much in the US. He only wanted to mention the places that he traveled out of the country cuz he didn't want to write me a textbook.

I responded back that I would love to travel with you one day. You seem like a very fun person to travel with.

He said that he was really a fun person to travel with. Because he travels mostly now by himself but he meets people all the time and everywhere he goes because he's a very sociable person and loves to laugh. And he loves the fact that Lady E, messaged him first. Honeydew said, his dad told him a long time ago, its not who you want, its who wants you….. so, thank you, for messaging honeydew first.

I told him that I was on social media dating site because I wanted to eventually get married. And in his social media dating profile stated he was divorced. I asked him would he get married again?

He responded " In a New York Minute",,, absolutely, marriage is a great thing. Especially when you have two people who have common goals. And it seems like we have one goal in common already. We are off to a great start. We want to travel and see the world. But there's only one condition. When I get married again the young lady must be willing to sign a prenuptial agreement and a postnuptial agreement.

I responded to him that, I was dating for love and I wanted to marry for love.

He responded to me well that's great, getting married for love but if Honeydew gets married again those are his conditions.

Honeydew also responded back to me and said that he had read my social media dating profile and notice that I was a Nurse Practitioner. He said that I should be making north of 200k a year. Have you ever heard of "a nurse with a purse". And if you're really truly and honestly considering marriage, you should absolutely want a prenuptial and a postnuptial agreement. Because money exposes real love and fake love.

Honeydew wished me the best in my dating adventures and said if you change your mind on the prenuptial agreement and postnuptial agreement, he gave me his three 1 three number and told me, give him a call.

A couple days went past and I didn't hear from him over the social media dating site. I talked to one of my girlfriends who is also a nurse. I told her that I met a guy on a social media dating site and he said that he was open to getting married again but he just required a prenuptial and post nuptial. My girlfriend said...girl that's a good thing. He ain't out here for your money. Just as some women are out here for men's money ...there's some men out here that are out here for women's money. So call him.

So, I did. I got right straight to the point and asked so why are you single, why are you divorced.

He said that there's one thing that he's learned in 44 years of living. Tell somebody the worst about you and see who sticks around. Check your phone..

While we were on the phone Honeydew stated ......that he had just sent me his divorce decree from his first divorce, divorce decree from his second divorce, where he filed for both divorces....also Honeydew sent court documents of State of Michigan vs 2nd X-wife, subpoenas, criminal conviction of second x- wife, for making false statements, to the police.. Honeydew also sent me his clear background check.

Honeydew stated you can fact check me for your own records or just trust me... I will never lie or mislead you.Tell someone the worst about you and see who sticks around. "now, do you still wanna stick around"? I, lady E, said, yes!!!

Honeydew said "I sent those documents because its all public information... and my Honeydew wanted to be HOT with me"...

In my head I thought, this is way too early for Honeydew to be trying to get fresh with me, especially on the phone and our first conversation.. So I told Honeydew to "slow down tiger"   Honeydew just laughed...and said you haven't seen a tiger yet...but you don't know what "HOT" means......I said no. Honeydew said "I want our relationship to be very.....very.......hot...hot.....hot.. I want us to be Honest,,,,, Open,,,,, Transparent.... HOT.....

Now....... Did that get you hot????? I laughed and got quiet.

Honeydew said ....Let's make a bet..

If you can spell Mississippi... in less than 6 seconds........We never have to talk again....

But if you can't spell Mississippi in less than 6 seconds......You do have to go out on a date with me.

You pick the place and I'll pick up the bill.

So what's it going to be Lady E......do we have a deal. I said yes. So Honeydew said.... "and the time clock starts now".

Of course, I cannot spell Mississippi in less than 6 seconds. And even if I could..... I was going to get it wrong anyways because I wanted to go out on a date with my Honeydew.

6 seconds came up and Honeydew said......"ding, ding, ding, ding, ding, you're out of time   you owe me a date tomorrow at 8pm.........You pick the place and I'll pick up the bill.

And the way you spell Mississippi......is...."M",..."I",.... crooked letter, crooked letter,......"I",....crooked letter,.....crooked letter,..." I",..... hump back, hump back,....."I",.....and started laughing....I laughed too...

Honeydew said my uncles used to sing that all the time as a kid in the 80's while sippin in Mississippi.

Again I ...laughed...

I said okay......Fishbones in Michigan. Honeydew said "right on sista... Fishbones is one of my favorite restaurants. They have an amazing "Oyster Rockefeller".

Honeydew then said "I have another call on the other line that I must take. And you will see me tomorrow". I said hold on wait a minute....you didn't tell me what you do for a living?

Honeydew said "what I earn for a living is legal...... I'm wholesome, I drink whole milk, I know you would like some chocolate milk......Your safe with me lil mama.... You don't have to look over your shoulder. You just must keep your head on a swivel from my two ex-wives. And Honeydew laughed out loud and said he'll talk to me tomorrow at 8:00 p.m. at Fish Bones..

I told my Honeydew I wasn't drinking… he said its ok… He'll order me a shot of water on the rocks. I laughed.. and we got off the phone….

13

Chapter 2

First Date

Our First Kiss, How To Make Sweaters For Mice

I was about 15 minutes late to our first date at 8pm….So I pulled up, parked, hopped out of my vehicle and started walking extremely fast through the parking lot of fish bones..

Then I heard someone yell out…. "Lady E",…… I turned around and saw this very, very, very handsome black young brother. He had full head of curly but short hair. A well-groomed goatee, a absolute beautiful bright smile, I notice, he had on camel hair sports coat, black t-shirt, black pants and black boots….. Honeydew was standing between the driver's door of a hard top convertible old school, that sounded like loud thunder rumbling at idle… I had no idea what that car was, but the car was shaking as it idled..

Honeydew shut his car off and ran quickly up to me, with his hand on the heat, and said "is somebody chasing you"? I said no… I'm late for our date Mr. and its cold as hell out here . Honeydew was like…… oh…. you know when you see people running ….you gotta run with them…… get to the safe place and then ask "why the hell you running"…. So honeydew grabbed my hand and we took off running.

We ran into Fishbones and we both started laughing, catching our breath…… once we got inside..

Again he made me laugh.

He smelled Absolutely amazing … He smelled like a clean breeze of beach sun screen, tropical fruit with the hint of fresh cut wood smell.. and coco butter… I told honeydew he smelled good. He said he took a shower instead of taking a hoe bath. Again he made me laugh….

We got inside the Fish bones restaurant…..it was completely empty…. Honeydew asked me where would I like to sit. I said the bar is fine… So we both headed to the bar. We got to the bar and he asked me…may I take your coat off for you…..there still gentlemen left out here. I looked at my honeydew….smiled and said sure… Honeydew slowly unzipped my coat, moved closer and whispered in my ear …. Can you turn around so I can remove your coat…I turned around, and he took my coat off   He then pulled out my chair for me.. Honeydew asked me, would you like to sit… Honeydew said……get ready for a roller coaster ride, and then he pushed my chair in, violently in closer to the bar..

Again I laughed.

So of course I said, you look very nice on your dating profile picture… they do not do you, any justice.. Honeydew responded… You're very attractive as well, and your dating profile pictures don't do you, any justice… I am such a lucky man to be graced with your presence…. You're a breath of fresh air..

I told Honeydew…. you made me laugh so hard when I read on your profile that you knitted sweaters for mice. I thought about that all day before I sent you that message…. Honeydew stated that He always looks at life as the funniest experience…..and everything has humor, and comedy, in it…even the worst situations….And he says he's really into quotes….Honeydew said he never takes life too serious, you're never going to make it out alive… we laughed.

Again I laughed……

I said I know that's right…So tell me how does one become a person who knits sweaters for mice…..

He let me know that his family had been knitting sweaters for mice since the early1800's…….his family also owns acres and acres of land in Mississippi to grow timber, Pecans and walnut trees.

He has a family inheritance and that is his inheritance….

Honeydew also said he will love to take me to Mississippi to see the land and process…

Honeydew also said his mother worked at a location in Michigan that had mice. And when she took her bag to work, sometimes the mice would get in her bag unknowingly. And then she would bring her bag home which had the mice. So his dad would ask his mother to leave her bag in the foyer when she came home from work. Then once the mice jumped out the bag. It would head to the cheese on the trap. Which would catch a mouse. His dad would take a napkin and cover up the mouse. He would show us how to do this as kids. When we were kids, his dad would say to the mouse, "Hey little fella, sorry it had to end like this, I'm gonna put this sweater on you, take you on out, its cold outside, poured the mouse a shot of whiskey from his cup, took the mouse outside and release the mouse in the street from the trap. His dad said put a napkin/sweater on the mice, because mice look for warm places to hide in the winter. So this happened often in the winter months here in Michigan. But never in the summers. So he got the joke of knitting sweaters, for mice from his dad. And in their house when his dad said that he had to knit a sweater for a mouse. Or whose turn is it to go put that sweater on the mouse. We all would laugh. His mother was terrified of mice. Even though she grew up on a farm with tons of field mice. But that's where honeydew got that expression from.

Honeydews dad was a very funny young man. He always kept his mother laughing. He would always tell people, when they say, the early bird gets the worm. Well just wait, the second mouse gets the cheese. Honeydew said, I think I got the cheese with you. Honeydew said he wishes I could have met his father. He was a real cool cat. Honeydew talked about his dad and how pivotal he was in making honeydew the man he is today. He told me that his dad was very light skinned and had ginger colored hair, with hazel eyes, always laughing. When they would go out to eat as a family. Waitresses would say, oh my God you have such beautiful eyes. His dad would say thank you, its how I was born and conceived in the islands. The waitresses say, well.....what island. And my dad would say belle Isle. And we would all laugh. His dad taught him how to be a gentleman and how to treat a lady. And he would sample that by how he treated honeydew's mother, his wife of 46 years. She never opened doors, honeydews dad did, his dad was always the provider but he let his mother be in control sometimes. Honeydew said that his dad told him that he must be the provider for the family and hold it together like the cement that holds the brick. His dad told him that he was the house. But his mother was the thermostat. And depending on her temperature it can make the house very cold or very hot. Sometimes you know you're going to be right. But knowing that you're right is easy. Real power is self-control, knowing that your right, knowing that you have the power, but when and where to use it. And sometimes real power involves you just walking away when you know your right.

Honeydew said I noticed you're driving a newer model Suv...Is that your main car.....Because I see you have a set of German luxury keys on your keychain. I told Honeydew that my Suv is my second vehicle..I really don't get a chance to drive my other luxury vehicle.... Because I'm in the field all day.... That's why I was late to our date...So I have this suv as my second vehicle....Not to put a lot of miles on my luxury vehicle..

Honeydew said he totally understood... He doesn't drive all of his family inherited vehicles either.. I asked what type of car is that outside.....its really loud.... Honeydew said that's not a car... that's the beast.... It has an all-aluminum V10 engine.... manual stick shift .....skirts in 3rd gear....with straight cat back exhaust...stupid fast...... all original all numbers matching.......

He only pulled the beast out tonight to impress me...I told him.. he didn't have to do that...... Its November...I wasn't one of those women that are impressed by flashy things that men have.....He said he knows... But first impressions are lasting impressions....and all the vehicles his family owns are not flashy... there classics...... Plus I needed to drive the beast.... She's been sitting marinating for too long.... wait till you see my families other vehicles... My family really love cars... Sometimes when I drive..... I don't even cut the radio on....I'd just like to listen to the Roar of the engine...

So I asked him, what happened for him to file for divorce in your marriages?

He said well, I had to learn how to bob and weave.. I said, you mean like, boxing, Honeydew was like yeah... Honeydew said his ex-wives were great people and beautiful stories. They just weren't made for the same book anymore and he wishes them wealth and success.

I said what are you doing to these women to make them want to hit you……Then honeydew said that he was being too nice. When you give someone everything they only want more. Sometimes when you treat people very nice they start to take your kindness for weakness……and try to take advantage of you…. Then when you begin to pull your kindness back and they see that life will continue to be great for you regardless of them….they get salty and upset.

Most people…. not all…. like to yell when they don't get their way…….Some people not all, like to throw things when upset…. Honeydew said, he swears one of his ex-wives was a back-up pitcher for the Detroit Tigers, and laughed. Some people not all, like to act out violently in aggression and hit…

And that's what his ex-wife's did…. So Honeydew said…. That's why he walked away and filed for divorce….

Honeydew said that he doesn't like to argue…. Were adults, we should be able to communicate and talk to each other… peacefully and respectfully.. I will listen to your side….I will tell you my side…then somewhere we have to ….meet in the middle….come to a mutual agreement… agree or agree to disagree…But it's very hard to talk to somebody when they're yelling at the top of their voice…

Aint nobody got time for that…. Honeydew said, Simply put… you give some one a inch…they will take a mile. You give a mouse a cookie crumb, he will want the whole cookie soon, and walk right on to a trap to get it.

I asked my Honeydew well, didn't you see some red flags.. In hindsight, Honeydew said his second x-wife's red flag 1 and 2 ..all happened in the same day…But red flag 3 was later on. But he was just blinded by 2nd x-wife not having kids… Honeydew being in his early 30's with no kids…and successful, but him wanting kids. My Honeydew ignored the signs.. Because he didn't want to deal with baby daddy drama from the women he was attracting in his early 30's who had children already.

Honeydew said, first…….let me say, I had to learn to forgive myself. That was the hardest part, filing for divorce was easy and gratifying. But what I mean by forgive myself is. Out of all the women, I could have had children with, I chose my 2nd x-wife when she showed so many red flags.

There were so many great young ladies who had children, that were successful and could have been great mothers to his children and my Honeydew passed them by, just because they had children.. Honeydew admitted his mindset back then was flawed, back then.. But he was trying a different approach now..

So you ask what was some of the red flags that 2nd x-wife did.

Honeydew told me he had a lost and found box at his condo.. I said what is a lost and found box.. and why do you need that. He said when women would come over to his condo some of who were going through problems in there relationship….some who were single.. to get comfortable the women would remove their accessories, like necklaces, earrings, etc. and sit them around his condo….well, when they would leave the women would either forget items or leave their items there on purpose....

Honeydew told me the reason these women would leave it there is to mark their territory meaning if another woman comes in his condo and sees female bracelets, hair scruchys… or bonnet… she gonna ask Honeydew, who's is this.. which caused drama for him...

He said guys do the same thing.... I said oh do they... he said yeah…. you wanna know how they mark there territory, to let other men know he was there, to cause drama in a woman's life....

I wanted to hear thIs... I told honeydew, cuz ain't no guys left anything at my house... I pay that rent…….

Honeydew looked at me dead in the eye.... and said, three baby daddies.... and laughed out loud…… I laughed out loud too....We laughed and laughed and laughed....

I said wait a minute.... I have three children....I bust out laughing again...

Honeydew said, "I know………I just told you", Honeydew grabbed his stomach, and laughed so hard he stopped breathing, he began sliding slowly out his high top bar chair like a worm, and started laughing hysterically, holding on to the bar with one hand……trying to stand up straight...honeydew   couldn't even get the words out... because he was laughing so hard....

We both went back to laughing for about a good...5 minutes   I used the napkins from under my water to wipe away tears from laughing so hard..

The waitress came over because we were laughing and said, in a slang,....." no, no, , ... yall over here having way, way too, much fun....laughing to, hard... what yall two over ha, ha and key keying.... about... I wanna laugh too...." in a joking way..

Honeydew.... still struggling to stand.... laughing   one hand on his stomach the other holding on to the bar.... said... trying to catch his breath.... took his hand off the bar... and pointed at himself....

I got 2 kids, and two divorces.... my 2nd x wife tried to ruin me... beat me...tried. to get me, and my best friend, locked up.. Honeydew was still laughing.... pointing at himself..

Then he started pointing at me still crying laughing....

She.... shee.... sheeee...sheee ....Honeydew struggling to get out his words between laughing... she ... shee... sheee.... just found out she has three baby daddies.....

The waitress hollered laughing ...... we all were laughing...

My Honeydew just made me laugh at my own situation.... that I always felt bad about...

After we stopped laughing, I told honeydew my children ages. I have a 22-year-old, a 20 year old, and a 10 year old. Honeydew said his children's ages were 6 and 10. We should play the midday and evening Lotto. Again I laughed. Honeydew said, girl you look 21, show me some ID... How do you have a 22-year-old. Again, I laughed.

So we went back to talking about red flag number 1, 2 and 3... Honeydew said red flag 1 happened and he didn't know it then but in hindsight... he knew it now..

So the lost and found box that he had at his condo contained a lot of bracelets earrings scrunchies hair pins you name it. It was in the lost and found box. When he had gotten with his second ex-wife in the dating phase. She asked him about this lost and found box when she came over to his condo. He let her know it was a lost and found box of items that other women had left over. He asked her if that bothered his 2nd x-wife. 2nd x-wife said no. 2nd x-wife said she was actually going to dig in here find the good stuff and where it.

Honeydew said he and his 2nd x-wife laughed about her wearing other women's items she got out the lost and found box.

That was flag number one. Wearing other people items that didn't belong to her.

About a couple months went by and my honeydew and his second ex-wife had not done the Lord's work. So my honeydew said that they went out one night and when they came back to his condo he let her know that he respected her decision about not doing the Lord's work, but he wanted to move on. 2nd x-wife then began to say that she was a good woman with no kids, and can be a great house wife and she was happy that Honeydew respected her decision. But 2nd x-wife asked, why give up on their relationship, just because 2nd x-wife wouldn't do the Lord's work. My honeydew said he told his 2nd ex-wife at the time, that he was a young man and he had multiple other female friends. And these other female friends wanted to do the Lord's work quite often.

And it would be wrong of Honeydew to try to be in a relationship with his second ex-wife and still be out there doing the Lord's work. So as his second ex-wife gathered her belongings to leave his condo because she has some articles of clothing at his condo. She picked up the whole lost and found box and took it with her. Honeydew said those are other people's things. 2nd x-wife said, they're my things now and walked out the door.

That was flag number 2. Keeping other peoples things that didn't belong to her.

So honeydew said that during that first disagreement, Honeydew had a female friend text him asking him if he was free.

Honeydew text back to his female friend, yes sure come on over, I have company that's about to leave. So Honeydew walked his second ex-wife to her vehicle. 2nd x-wife said again, your really making a big mistake.. your gonna regret this… I don't have any kids, you don't have any kids and a very successful black man in your early 30's and I'm a young woman who can be an awesome house wife.

I just want to wait to be married before I do the Lord's work. Honeydew said to his 2nd x-wife, I think I'm making the right decision. As he opened the door for his 2nd ex-wife for her to get into the car and put her belongings in the car.

His other female friend pulled up. Honeydew female friend saw that he was talking to his 2nd x-wife. She politely pulled into one of honeydew's multiple parking spots under the carport.

Honeydew left his second ex-wife, wished her the best and went over to the other car. Open the door for his other female friend and gave her a big hug and they walked into his condo.

His second ex-wife had not pulled off yet. About 2 weeks went by and honeydew received a call from his second ex-wife. She said she just wanted to talk and asked to come over… I'm around the corner from your Condo.

Honeydew said you can come over, but you can't come in, to his 2nd x-wife. We can sit by the pond and talk. 2nd x-wife came and they talked. She asked who was that female friend that I walked in my condo with. Honeydew said, a female friend. What did you guys do. I told her, the Lord's work. 2nd x-wife then got upset. Why would you do that, I thought we were doing good. Honeydew said to his 2nd x-wife that…you're the one who called me to come back over to my condo…. Why did you call me.. you could have kept driving. I was perfectly fine with not seeing you again.

Honeydew said to his 2nd x-wife I was honest with you and instead of lying to you, I respected you decision to want to wait to do the Lord's work till your married. I asked you to leave my crib. But as for me and my condo, I'm gonna do the lord's work. That's why I asked you to leave so my other female friend could come over. Honeydew said that his 2nd x-wife said that she didn't want honeydew to leave her or hurt her if they did the Lord's work… she has been hurt, so many times in the past before. And asked to come back up to honeydew condo.

Honeydew then said, his 2nd x-wife asked him to go up to his condo. That was red flag number 3. Why is it that for 2 months honeydew 2nd x-wife didn't do the Lord's work. And just by her seeing Honeydew walking another young lady into his condo. Now you want to do the Lord's work.

That was red flag number three..

And let me start by saying……. giving those divorce papers was so gratifying …finally I was done with my **Escape Plan, and free**. Honeydew said, he C-walked, all the way out the house…

After being punched in the face… that was the last straw…he pulled out his phone and he showed me a picture of himself the next morning with a newspaper up to his face in the mirror… with dark bruises, and a contusion lump on the left side of his face…and ring camera videos of the incident..

I said…… Honeydew…… noooo….. why didn't you call the police……. Honeydew chuckled…. and said… *I needed her to keep her job…* and it was all part of an **Escape Plan**……

So what type of plan involves….you getting the shit beat out of you by a girl……… cause it looks like she whipped your ass on that picture… and that ring camera video too…. I laughed out loud and so did my honeydew….

It was an **Escape Plan** that helped me to lower my child support from $4200 a month, down to $800 a month.

Honeydew said, I'll tell you about my **Escape plan**… But before our food comes out, he asked me did I know how to ballroom dance or step? I said no….he said that he used to teach a class back in the day, when he first started knitting sweaters from mice. He said I could show you how to cut the rug, and step before our food comes out. The restaurant is empty, so nobody's really looking to see if you step on my feet.

Again he made me laugh.

I said sure. Honeydew said let me pull out your seat. Honeydew pulled out my seat and extended out his left hand, I held his left hand and he walked me behind my seat.

He said in order for me to show you how to dance, he had to put his hands on my hips. Cuz when you ballroom dance sometimes you have to gently push a woman from her hips to start a 360 degree turn.

He asked, is it okay if I touch your right hip. I promise, I won't go no lower. I'm not trying to get slapped on our first date. He let out a big laugh and I laughed as well…

Again he made me laugh..

So with the background music that they were playing in the restaurant, he said it's all about staying on beat. So he lined me up with him and started to rock, as he held my hips and gently pushed my hips to match his hips and then we just started rocking together.

Honeydew then brushed my hair over my ear and whispered into my ear..

Can I kiss you on the lips. I promise I'm not going in for full tongue action....I'm talkin, just like a little chicken peck action...Just like lil,, cute harmless baby yellow chicken picking up bird seed. I just want a lil nibble....thats all.... I know you aint gonna let this lil chicken not get fed...That's animal cruelty.... And I will report you... I'm starving over here.....I feel that this is the right time and I won't get this moment again. Throw some bird seed out for me. ......And then he pushed back from my hips and bent over and laughed to himself. Which made me laugh cuz he has a very very very funny laugh.

Then honeydew held me, I pulled my hair back and looked honeydew straight in his eyes, and said why did you even have to ask to kiss me, you should have just did it.

Honeydew said, well all right sista. I'm going to go in and pick up this bird seed, on the count of three. 1, 2, and kissed me on count two. That was our first kiss. We enjoyed the rest of the night laughing, and eating good food. All the way up until they told us the bar manager said, hey it looks like you guys are having a great time, but we have to close. We didn't know but we had been there from 8:00 p.m. all the way to 2:00 a.m. laughing and joking. Just us, in an empty restaurant.

So they handed us the bill. Honeydew said loudly, I got this   he pulled out a roll of pennies and asked me, I hope I don't embarrass you by paying for our meal in pennies, but that's all the little mice can carry to pay for the sweaters that we make for them....He let out a loud laugh, which made me laugh, even the waitress and manager....

I told honeydew he keeps on making me laugh.

Even before I met him. He had me laughing and thinking about him.

He said, well, let's keep this train rolling. He had already greased the tracks, and he knew an after hours joint that we could hit so he can finish teaching me how to ballroom dance and step. And honeydew said he had a babysitter.

I told him I would love to hang out with him but I had to get home and go to bed. I have clients I have to see early in the morning. But I asked him what are you doing tomorrow. He said, I'm doing you. He let out a big laugh and I laughed too. Again he made me laugh.. I said let's get out of here, can you walk me to my car. Honeydew paid the bill, held my hand and walked me to my suv.

Honeydew said, I have to start the beast and let it run for a while before I start driving it. These older cars you can't just hop in them and drive, you got to let them run for a minute, you got to warm it up. He started his old school. And it sounded like somebody was letting off thunderous fireworks. I asked honeydew... is the beast supposed to sound like that. He was like yes... this is what you call a cold start, I love that rumbling popping sound.

He opened the door to my suv which was already running and warm because of the auto start. I squeezed my honeydew and laid a big kiss on him. And told him he could wait in my car, its already warm, while his is warming up. So he got me in on the driver side and he walked around to the passenger side. And I leaned over and opened the door for him.

As soon as he got in the car, honeydew said thank you. I said for what. He said that normally girls don't do that, lean over, and open up the door for the dude, type thing. That just shows that I was a good person and he really wanted to see me tomorrow and would cancel all of his plans and his mice sweater orders and shipping, just to spend one minute with me.

Then I started kissing my honeydew again. I stopped and said, hey as much as I would love for this to continue. I think I should go before I get myself in trouble.

Honeydew laughed and said, I just want to come up and talk. Is that all right. He laughed and I laughed. I said yeah, that's all right. I'll call you in the car while you're driving...

So the next morning I told him I had a Keurig and I wanted green tea. He was free to make himself whatever… I had, in the carousel tree, coffee, tea and apple cider..

My Honeydew asked me what are my goals for today. I said see about 10 to 8 clients and then come back and see you. He said right on sista. Honeydew said he had to knit some more sweaters for mice and his sewing machine went down. So he was going to have to get some tweezers and fix it. And let out a big laugh and so did I. Again he made me laugh. Honeydew asked me so what do you want tonight to eat. I said I don't know, I picked last time. I, Lady E, said, you pick a place I'll pick up the bill… Honeydew said, I'm no cheap date… He could really eat and didn't want to run up a huge bill for Lady E to pay and have to wash dishes. I told my Honeydew…. you pick a place I'll pick up the bill, I got you…What's your favorite restaurant. Honey dew said, I'm the second mouse, I just got the cheese. You just reciprocated… I took honeydew to his favorite restaurant, Taco Bell… and we ordered off the dollar menu.

Chapter 3

Honeydew Escape Plan

I Needed Her to Keep Her Job

Read this chapter and the next chapter if you just want to see how honeydew used his own Escape Plan. But to really understand your Escape Plan, start at page 1.

So on our first date I asked my Honeydew….so what type of plan involves….you getting the shit beat out of you by a girl……. cause it looks like she whipped your ass on that picture… and that ring camera video…. I laughed out loud and so did my honeydew he said, it was all part of his **Escape Plan…*I, needed her, to keep her, job*.** My honeydew told me his Escape Plan on our first date. He also said when I tell you this. Don't judge me… I made it out safe and still successfull..

Now, understand my Honeydew is very honest with me. He said he was nervous about filing for divorce and if his **Escape Plan** was going to work. Honeydew said, he was even more successful after his first divorce. He had a pre-nup. But he was still nervous. That prevented him from filing for divorce way earlier because he was afraid. He didn't know what the future held. He knew that he had an **Escape Plan**. But this was something that he had not done in his life before. But my honeydew listened to something on the radio that influenced him and some Bible verses. And nothing beats a fail, but a try, every day.

Honeydew was listening to a radio host say, he walked away from his mansion because he didn't want to be with the young lady that he was married to anymore. He knew he could get another mansion again.

The question was, could she get another mansion? Because he was the one who got them in their first mansion on his biz. He was in the biz. But his soon to be x-wife wasn't a biz.

Honeydew pulled out the Bible on his cell phone. A Bible verse just rang out in his head that he had heard millions of times before. But it just kept ringing in his head. Proverbs 21:9, Proverbs 25:24, Proverbs 27:15, All those verses pretty much state the same thing. It is better to dwell in a corner of a rooftop than in a house with a quarrelsome wife.

My honeydew heard that quiet still small voice in his gut that said, it's time to pull the trigger. And put his plan into motion. Honeydew knew that he had come this far by faith. Honeydew also knew that he was in the mice making sweater business. Honeydew can get this all over again when he walks away. But can his second ex-wife?

Sometimes and often to get out of the storm, you must go through the storm or read about people who made it out of their self-inflicted storm. You can become a self-inflicted masterpiece.

Honeydew activated his plan. It was a plan that helped my honeydew to lower his child support from $4200 a month down to $800 a month, Honeydews severance package. Not having to pay alimony and little child support for 2 children. Honeydew said, the seven-year itch or the half-life of the marriage concept. Basically, all it is that, when a couple files for divorce. You add up the number of years that they've been married and just divided by two. The midpoint is when husband or wife was ready to file for divorce.

In Honeydew situation with his second ex-wife, they were together and married for 11 years.

So at five and a half years into their marriage honeydew was ready to file for divorce the first time his 2nd x-wife put her hands on him. So he went to his family attorney and they ran the numbers of what his second x-wife would get if he was to file for divorce.

But he had to understand some hard numbers and the truth. Reality set in. 18 years paying child support and a lifetime of paying alimony. Even though honeydew signed a prenuptial agreement with the second ex-wife. He needed a second level of verification so he would not have to pay alimony or high child support. You have to know your opponent, he had been fooled once….. on his first marriage, hence the pre-nup for second marriage. Honeydew told me that when he knew his divorce was over he had to expect his second ex-wife to do the worst. But he was praying for her to do the best. But just in case she did the worst he had a **Escape Plan** for that.

My honeydew's family inheritance and mice making sweater biz was making significantly more than what his second ex-wife made. So when he knew that he was ready for divorce. But didn't want to pay alimony or high child support. His 2nd x-wife could try to fight to invalidate the pre-nup. He had to think of his **Escape Plan**. My honeydew knew he couldn't act off emotion and just file for divorce. Honeydew said he had to appear as a sheep…. Until he had to show he can be a wolf in sheepskin….

My honeydew played a song for me on our first date that dealt with drinking a coconut flavored rum drink….I've heard people sing the hook to the song before. But I never fully took the time to listen to the whole song. Listen to that song in it's entirety and you'll get a good laugh.

So five and a half years into the marriage, my honeydew knew his marriage was going to fail….. he didn't say anything to his second ex-wife he just started to work on his **Escape Plan**..

Honeydew didn't say anything to some of his closest associates for two reasons, he felt embarrassed and fearful that honeydew **Escape Plan** was going to get back to his second ex-wife. Honeydew said, his associates were like old refrigerators, couldn't keep nothing. LOL,

Honeydew maintained a calmful cheerful smile and continued to be the best husband that he knew. But he knew his **Escape Plan** was going to take about 5 to 6 years to work out. Which would allow Honeydew to continue to build and create for himself in the storm. All honeydew had to do was, weather the storm. Sometimes you have to be comfortable, being uncomfortable.

Here's what my honeydew did know… he knew how much his family inheritance was. He knew how much his second ex-wife made. Honeydew encouraged his second ex-wife to go back to college and finish getting her bachelor and then go back to get her masters…. Honeydew did this with purpose…. Honeydew paid on his 2nd x-wife student loans to get her financial aid back active again, paid for her books, helped her study for her test by writing out note cards and quizzing her encouraging her to continue to go to school when she wanted to quit. Honeydew went to counseling with his 2nd x-wife and paid for it out of pocket and with insurance. Honeydew acted as if he wanted the marriage to work, all the while knowing it was going to fail. Honeydew knew that he didn't need counseling to get his 2nd x-wife…and counseling was not going to save them.

When someone has a history of being a certain way…trust that is the way their going to be, for the rest of their lives. And its not for you to waste your time trying to fix them. Its your job to fix yourself and prepare for this imminent attack from a known enemy and brace for impact. Know your opponent.

Honeydew appearing as a supportive husband wanting to help his 2nd x-wife to better herself. Staying at home watching the kids while 2nd x-wife took online classes, and went to college campus, going to graduation ceremonies… And what do you know, the shit worked… his second ex-wife ended up getting her masters degree. And Honeydew motivated his 2nd x-wife to quit her current job that she was working because now she had a master's degree that made her more marketable for employers. Honeydew encouraged his 2nd x-wife to take a better job.

Honeydew did that because he knew if you have elevated you're soon to be ex-husband or soon to be ex-wife to a level of comfortability or standard of living. And if you file for divorce, alimony will apply to you as well as child support if you make more than the other spouse. Honeydew said his 2nd x-wife told him from jump, that she didn't want to work for the rest of her life. She wanted to stay at home and be a good kept house wife and take care of her husband and kids. That was cool then, but hell no now. Honeydew knew his opponent.

But honeydew knew that if you encourage your soon to be ex-husband or soon to be ex-wife to better themselves by going back to school graduating and getting a better job they are considered now gainfully employed, and once gainfully employed, that is all taken into account when you file for divorce. So honeydew encourage his 2nd x-wife to start a business too….There's no way you're soon to be ex-husband or soon to be ex-wife can ask for alimony because they're gainfully employed and they can sustain their quality of life without you having to give money. Now, honeydew already had a prenuptial agreement that stated no alimony. But just to have a 2nd backup plan, because the system is flawed, he pushed his second ex-wife to better herself so she will be gainfully employed so when honeydew filed for divorce he knew that his second ex-wife counterclaim too divorce would be to ask full physical and legal sole custody of the children and alimony, to sustain their way of living, Which she did. Know your opponent.

But what honeydew 2nd x-wife did not know is that, she would not be able to get alimony because she was gainfully employed now…. It was documented that, She could start and successfully run a business from honeydews idea and capitol. And honey do just stay behind the scenes. Even though honeydew paid all the bills and she was just able to stack her money. When it came down time to it, his soon to be second ex-wife could afford all the bills because now honeydew encourage her and paid for her to go back to school, get her financial aid cut back on and get a her a better job and get her paid more.

Now tell me that ain't gangster. A five and a half year magic trick that worked. now You See Me Friend of the court, Now you don't.

His second ex-wife did try to fight him in court to invalidate the prenup. My honeydew thought of that as well.

With her going back to school and finishing her bachelor's and then going back to school right after and getting her Masters, racking up a huge student loan bill, that Honeydew paid to get back active…. Honeydew helped her start a biz. Honeydew encouraged 2nd x-wife to max out what she could invest in her retirement plan a 401k. Now just as 2nd x-wife was trying to invalidate the prenuptial agreement. Because she had a 401k. And because she had got a better job that hubby influenced her to get. Because honeydew paid all the bills for the house with 2nd x-wife. She was able to stack all her money from her better job. Honeydew encouraged her to put all that money into her 401k. And he would take care of everything else. So honeydews second ex-wife decided to max out the amount that she could put into her 401k.

Now what his 2nd x-wife didn't know was just as she was trying to fight to invalidate the prenuptial agreement. Honeydew could go after her large 401k. That he motivated and told her to max out. Because honeydew was paying all the bills at the house, her car note, insurance, cell phone bill, etc.

So that was also Honeydews second layer of protection for his future. If his second ex-wife wanted to fight him to invalidate the prenuptial agreement. Then honeydew would take half of her 401k. Which was a lot of money. And his second ex-wife would not get alimony because she was gainfully employed and lose half of her 401k.

So now his second ex-wife had to really sit and think. Do I want to give up half of my stuff. Like I'm trying to take half of his. His second ex-wife took a knee in court, stood down and gave full cooperation to honeydew, if she wanted anything..

She understood that she lost…. And she recognized she lost.. the moment honeydew gave her the divorce paperwork. Honeydew said, he checked all his 2nd ex-wife financials to make sure all her money was still in the accounts, he laid the divorce papers down on the table with her financials and said. Now you can either fight to invalidate the prenup which I know you will do…. But understand this, who pushed you to go back to college, who pushed you not to be a housewife and be an independent woman out here. Who helped you grow your bank account to that amount. Who encourage you to max out what you can put in your 401k.

Now I have helped you better yourself, you used to complain about how little you made. Now you have the ability to make close to six figures and to make more. I just want out of this marriage.

Honeydew said to his 2nd x-wife, "I knew and saw your defense a long time ago". I saw your defensive front line called "mother in-law, brother(broke attorney) and retired dad", your linebackers called "Child Support", your defensive ends called "hating girlfriends", your safety named "alimony" set way back deep. I had to call the audible sista… ….

Honeydew stood up, on our first date, put his hand under the bar high top seat, like he was a quarterback, and the bar seat was the center…… Honeydew shouted out….red 18, ,,,,,,,,,red 18,…….wait, wait, wait….. its Child Support out there and alimony in the back field…. That's man to wallet coverage defense….

While standing Honeydew shouted out. *Kentuuckyyyyyyyyyky,,, ……..Kentucky, Blue 42…blue 42……. sixty-nine, , sixty-nine, morning time ,,* and stomped his right foot on the ground …like he was playing football…and he was a quarterback calling the play. He, asked me to run around the back of him at the restaurant bar …. So I did… rolling, Laughing so hard…

Honeydew said he threw the football and let his 2nd x-wife intentionally catch the interception and let her run it in for a touchdown. But just one touchdown or homerun will not win the game. Honeydew had that bite, and grit, like the three1 three Lions and Tigers. No one is afraid of the roar, they're afraid of the bite.

So, try if you want to come for me then I will be forced to come for you. You will feel my bite; you're not going to want to come down off this mountain top, save your face sista. Don't cut off your nose to spite your face. I have the family inheritance to keep fighting in court, keep fighting in court, keep fighting in court and…………… keep fighting the court. Pretty soon you will wipe out all your money, lose everything, just trying to protect nothing that I will legally take. So, we can either go to mediation, keep what you have now, that I can get again tomorrow or you can fight in court. But I think you know I've already won, the ball is in your court, so it's your move next.

Its 4th quarter now, this game, you knew we were playing, has now turned from football, baseball, checkers, to chest. Your move….

But honeydew already knew it was checkmate..

And my Honeydew, C-walked it, out the house playing theme music on his blue tooth speaker and wearing chucks.

Right on son, as Honeydew dad would say. Thanks pops, for showing me, how to walk away when I know I'm right.

Chapter 4 Your Escape Plan

2 bananas and $109,900 stack of cash

Read this chapter if you just want to use the Escape Plan for a quick read. But to really understand your Escape Plan, start at page 1.

This is what you need to do. Start right now with what you have and where you're at. To those who are reading this book, every situation is different. Ex-wife or ex-husband can be your baby mama or baby daddy. Apply this **escape plan** to your situation, however it fits and applies. If you are in a domestic violence situation, call the domestic violence hotline. But honeydew can take a punch. Get knocked down and get back up. I have learned that about him, he will not quit, he will not give up, He's like a honey badger.

Assess your situation. If your soon to be x-husband or x-wife makes less than you, then help them and encourage them, by all means to better themselves… go back to school to get a degree so they can make more money, get a skilled trade so they can make more money, start a business so they can get more money, encourage them to invest a lot of the money they earn into 401k, stocks, bonds, whatever. Just make sure that income is documented and do you know the source.

This will be hard, but it is worth it. Because the more income your soon to be ex-husband or soon to be ex-wife or soon to be baby daddy or soon to be baby mama makes, the less you have to pay.

Contribute to prosperity, do good and help others, it shall be returned. Just as in equal amounts. Plant a good seed. For that, is the law of karma.

You must do this acting as a caring, supportive, loving spouse. All the while you know, that your planning your **Escape Plan**. Your ex doing better in life will be your bargaining chip when you file for divorce or leave.

For men or women who are currently married right now, who want to file for divorce or leave the person that they're with but don't want to get hit with high child support for the next 18 years or alimony for the rest of your life or until the person you divorced gets remarried. Believe it, women pay child support and alimony too.

What Honeydew knew. Child support only goes until the child is 18 years old. Alimony can last for the duration of that person's life or until they get remarried.

You just have to look at the numbers, would you rather get stuck paying high child support for the next 18 years. Or would you like to get stuck having to pay high alimony to your ex-husband or ex-wife for the rest of their life until they remarry. Just looking at the numbers you're sick and tired of your ex-wife or ex-husband right now. If you can't get along with them at this current point…. what makes you think somebody else will. So it's going to be a cold day in hell before they get remarried again. Then you have to look at the life expectancy of a male and a woman.

The average life expectancy of a man is 76.5 years. The average life expectancy of a woman is 81 and a half years. Just look at the numbers, 18 years of child support or a lifetime paying alimony to your ex-wife or ex-husband.

Believe that when someone has a history of being a certain way…trust that is the way they're going to be the rest of their lives. And it's not for you to waste your time trying to fix them. It's your job to fix yourself and prepare for this imminent attack from a known enemy and brace for impact. Know your opponent.

So, if you're at that point where you're ready to file for divorce from your soon-to-be ex-husband or soon to be ex-wife. Great, just get ready to have a plan that might have to last five and a half years. Give off the illusion that you're being supportive, and you want the best for your soon to be ex-wife or soon to be husband. But in reality, you understand that when you file for divorce, you're soon to be ex-wife and soon to be ex-husband have to be gainfully employed not to receive alimony and for you to pay low child support..

Now how to lower your child support that you will have to pay. It all depends on if you still want to see your children. That's the nuts and the bolts of it, that's the black and white of it. There is no grey. That's why the book text is black and white. And that is the real question. Do you still want to see your children?

And real talk. You just have to man up or woman up and take care of those kids, you brought these kids into the world. Those children did not ask to be here. So do what you legally need to do, to take care of those kids. They didn't ask to be here. But at the same time the system is flawed. So, you need to protect yourself because some amounts of child support and some amounts of alimony are just crazy. It doesn't take all that money to raise a child. What it takes is two parents who love their children wholeheartedly. Two parents who understand to the core what is in the best interest of their children. Is to Co parent. But sometimes you can't even do that. You just have to pay the price, child support, which you should pay, but not that much, and catch up with your youngins when they get older. And pray they make it in life without your guidance. And why should you have to pay alimony to somebody who has two feet, two hands and a mind and can do the exact same thing as you. If they just apply themselves. Why should your child support be higher than his or hers other baby mamas or other baby daddies just cause you have a family inheritance?

If you don't want to see your children, pay your child support, eat a donut with some chocolate milk, bucket of chicken, sit on the dock, fish, laugh and enjoy the day.

If you still want to see your children, then you need to start right now and get every picture/video that you have with your child from the day that they were born all the way up until today's date. Because you always prepare for the worst and pray for the best. And when you file for divorce or leave your soon-to-be ex-husband or soon-to-be ex-wife. You can expect that they're going to say that you are no good mother or no good father and ask for full custody of the children, so you have to pay more alimony and have to pay more child support. Trust, the child support and alimony will not go to the child.

But if you can show the court pictures and video that you have been in your children's life since they were born. That rebuts you're soon to be ex-wife or soon to be ex-husband claim that you were a deadbeat father or deadbeat mother. Thus, allowing you to get joint physical and legal custody of your children which will lower your child support. And you still get to see your children.

Now if you want to see your children, have joint custody, but have got to let your children go because you're ex-husband, ex-wife or baby mama, baby daddy, causing all types of drama and interfering in your new relationship, marriage and life. They want to cook you like a rotisserie chicken, lol... They don't want you to be happy because you left. LOL. And you would rather pay child support and just walk away, because it's easier, because you know you can accomplish more in your life without the drama of your ex-husband, ex-wife, baby mama, baby daddy. But you can't just give up your children for adoption or walk away because the biological parents can't co-parent, no matter how hard you tried. That's called child neglect. You must cut bait and set sail. You must have an **Escape Plan**.

You must prepare to lower your child support and give your children back legally. And honeydew thought of that and went through that too. Just know your child support will be slightly higher, but your life going forward will be great. Honeydew knew he was meant to soar and fly like eagles. But you have to experience turbulence to get above the clouds where the sun is always shining.

This is the turbulence, it's about to get bumpy. Stay on the course and go higher where the air is smooth. Honeydews attorneys, plural, because he has multiple attorneys, two and three heads are better than one if you can afford it. Honeydew had to fight to get joint custody of his children, Honeydew had to fight to give them back legally. Return to sender. Honeydew wants to save you attorney's fees, which are expensive and could wipe you out if you don't have a family inheritance to fall back on. So, listen up!!!

You must provide your children a safe place to live. But let's just say you have a mice problem. You must slowly document that you have called exterminators to get rid of this rodent problem. The exterminators have put out bait for the mice. Which if touched can be very toxic and life threatening to anybody. **So, anyone who has children can attest to this. When have you told your child to do something and they haven't. Document when you have told your children to do something and they didn't do it.** For example, cameras on the outside of your home for security that record video and audio. "I told the kids not to ride their bikes without their bike helmet, put your helmet on kids, for safety". Use that documentation to show the court your home location and your children might not do what you ask of them, they are children and you want them to be safe. File the paperwork with friend of the court to suspend your joint custody until your rodent problem is eradicated. Just because you suspend your joint custody. Doesn't mean you can't get it back, to spend time with your children, if you want. When you want to spend time with your children. It doesn't matter if it's a day, week, month years or decades till you file to get custody back. Ask yourself the question? How long does it take to get rid of mice? Once you put in the order to suspend your parenting time because of your rodent problem. It is suspended until you can show proof that your rodent problem has been eradicated. Then all you have to do………………when you want or feel like it.

And honeydew emphasizes when you want or feel like it. Get your kids back when you feel like it. When your situation is what you want it to be. You can always go back to court and file for joint custody. When you want and legally get joint custody because your joint custody is just suspended legally not terminated.

Friend of the court has to give custody to your ex-husband or ex-wife or baby mama or baby daddy because it's in the best interests of the children for the children's to be with the father or mother in a safe home. The children need a safe place to live with the gainfully employed mother or father. Now tell me that ain't gangster.

If you are a W-2 employee. You have to stop being a W-2 employee. But you just can't up and quit your W2 job. Cuz Friend of the Court will say, just because you up and quit your job. Because you want to lower your child support. Friend of the Court is going to say, you're still responsible for paying child support to your children or ex-spouse standard of living. The court will ask? Would you have quit your job if you weren't going through a divorce or on child support?. Go Find another job and they're going to continue to make you pay a high child support and tell you to find another job. And then when you're not paying for your child support you're going to stack up a huge bill with child support and alimony. They call it "arrears". That is unpaid child support and alimony that has accrued overtime. so let's say you're responsible for paying $1,000 a month. And you up and quit your w-2 job. You take another job. But you only can pay $100. The other $900 will be added to arrears. The court will say, find another high paying job and continue to charge you $1000.

That balance that you owe will go on your credit report and affect you from buying other things in the future. Arrears will cause you to lose your license, make you unable to get a passport and travel out the country , unable to get another job because now you have a criminal record for unpaid child support and alimony. Honeydew knows all about that. He had a very qualified male employee apply to work at his family inherited business to knit sweaters for mice. Trust, Honeydew, its hard to find a good man that wants to work making mice sweaters. Due to the powers that be, honeydew has to run a mandatory background check on all his employees. Upon running a background check it was discovered that the young man had a felony child support warrant. He advised the young man of this felony child support warrant and amount. The male applicant did not know of the felony child support warrant. Fully able to do the job but unable to get hired. Because of his felony child support warrant, honeydew was not able to give him a job working behind the sewing machine to knit sweaters for mice. That charge can even get you arrested. The court will threaten to lock you up. And the court will lock you up. Hence why, this system is so flawed. How can you get a job to pay your child support if you have a felony or misdemeanor child support warrant that stops you from getting a job. And it doesn't take all that money to raise a child.

But if your job or 1099, contractor employment lets you go or terminates you or fires you for medical reasons. And your medical reason stops you from working on your W-2 or 1099 job or any other job. Your child support and alimony has to be reduced because you can no longer physically do your job because of medical reasons. And you must sell it and I mean sell it good. Let everybody know because of your medical condition you cannot work. File all the proper paperwork with the court.

Look at the job that you're doing, it has tremendous wealth and potential.

You must look at this example.

Put 2 bananas on the left side of the table.

Put $109,900 in cash on the right side of the table.

Now hypothetically speaking let's just say you had a pet monkey.

What do you think your pet monkey is going to grab first. The 2 bananas or the stack of cash. Your pet monkey is going to grab the 2 bananas. But what your pet monkey is not intelligent enough to know that if he grabbed the cash, he could buy $109,900 worth of bananas... over time and never go hungry.

The 2 bananas is your W-2 job..

The stack of $109,900 cash is your 1099 job..

You have to work smarter, not harder.

You can do that same job but work for yourself. And make a grip. But you have to slowly convert from a W2 or 1099 contractor into a 1099 contractor that only makes 10% and have it documented. Because the 1099 contractor pay fluctuates. If you could prove that you only make 10% for about 2-3 years friend of the court must lower your child support because of medical reasons. Without the need of paying high-priced attorneys to fight your case. Just submit your proper forms, which is a modification of child support, your previous 2-3 years 1099 taxes showing low income. And if you haven't filed taxes in a while... its all good.. just file for the last 2-3 years.. the other years before , let the three letter government agency handle that. The main objective is to lower your child support. The court will handle the rest. You might not even have to go to court. Just have an address where you can receive mail and monitor it. Call the court periodically just to check on the status of your case. But you may have to go to court, because you're soon to be ex-husband, ex-wife, baby Mama, baby daddy, might file a motion with the court to review your 10% pay that you're receiving, once they see reduction in what they're getting. But as long as everything is documented. You're good to go.

Honeydew filed a modification of child support. Friend of the court lowered his child support. His ex-wife did not like the amount that friend of the court lowered it too. So, Honeydew received mail from friend of the court requesting a hearing. Honeydew forwarded that mail to his family paid attorneys. Who in turn subpoenaed his ex-wife financials. It was discovered that honeydews ex-wife was making a significant amount of money working three jobs now, after honeydew filed for divorce. When Honeydew's attorney advised her of this, Honeydew 2nd x-wife had to take another knee in court. The new amount that honeydew had to pay was a lot cheaper than the first amount friend of the court said honeydew had to pay because honeydews 2nd ex-wife falsified her income on the friend of the court affidavit, and she was making a lot more. Had honeydews 2nd ex-wife not requested a hearing, she would have been getting a lot more. You got to laugh at that one. Honeydew's attorney asked him how much child support did he want to pay, what do you think is fair for your children and in the best interests of your children. Honeydew **Escape Plan** worked. Honeydew got to choose how much he wanted to pay for child support. Because of friend of the court number was way low. Honeydew new his family mice sweater making business was only paying him 10%. Honeydew could prove it and document it for the court.. He could, and he did, Honey dew thought $400 a month would be cool for each of his youngins…

His child support was calculated to $367 a month from the court for both children.. So friend of the court isn't all that bad. There fair when you know the game… $800 a month is all he pays for child support instead of $4200 a month, the rest is history.

So what you do is, find someone you can trust or a best friend. And it really has to be somebody that you can trust that got your back no matter what… and can keep the secret to the grave, and not hang it over your head. Do not tell anyone about your **Escape Plan**, but just only the people, that need to know. And if they're truly honestly your best friend or truly honestly somebody that you trust, they already know your situation and they know that you're unhappy in your marriage or with your child's mother or father. And your best friend or the person who you really trust wants to see you happy and enjoy life to the fullest.. Start a LLC, C Corp or S Corp and put the person's name on it who you trust.

Do not put your name on it. Do not put your name on it. Do not put your name on it, or any bank account with your best friend or person that you trust. Friend of the court will look at that and call it, co-mingled accounts. So now if you do finally get surprised with a divorce from your soon to be ex-wife or soon to be ex-husband. Friend of the court cannot say your name is commingled with your best friend or person who you trust business account. Because what friend of the court will do is say that since your name it's on a business account that has brought in over $950,000 in a calendar year. That's a lot of mice sweaters…. They will attribute that to your income. They will then use that to dictate what your income is and that will raise your child support, and it will also raise your alimony. So do not put your name on anything or your Social Security number. Do not put your name on a house. Just sign a sub-lease with your best friend or person will you trust as the owner of the house and a small portion that you have to pay rent from the 10% you earn, that will be your rent. Do not put any vehicles, helicopters, yachts, airplanes, etc. in your name. Put it in your friends name or the person who you trust. Because friend of the court we'll look at your expenses and say that your expenses exceed the 10% that you're earning. The court will say that is a benefit from the 1099 job your working. They will use those numbers to dictate what your income is. Survive below your means. Meaning, act as if your begging for a mice sweater to stay warm, Until they find out, you own the mice sweater making company. This is where you really have to trust your best friend or person that you trust that has your back.

Sign a management contract with your best friend or the person that you trust. Update that management contract annually. Document it and save it for future purposes. Have them give you a 1099 each year for 10% of what that person who you trust or your best friend business makes. Then somewhere you guys meet up at the bar, coffee shop, ice cream shop, wherever it doesn't matter. something like that and take care of your business.

Work out a deal with your best friend or someone you trust for maybe for them to keep xxx% and also file taxes in your best friends or person who you trust name on The Business of all the income that it made. And then use the other xxx% to establish a line of credit for that business . Apply for credit cards for a secure line of credit under that business name.. Maybe buy a house or vehicles or a condo.. and you can use that as a business expense as a write-off because your best friend or person you trust needs those business expenses to continue to make the business run.

Buy a building or house for you under that business name, that can be turned into a home office. A vehicle that you drive that is under that business name can be used to conduct business to your customers. Restaurants vacations can be used to establish new business connections for your customers under that business name. It's a business and you want to attract more customers. So you just have to do everything legally and document if its for a business conference or business meeting or personal pleasure, just make sure you document it.

Continue to work your W-2 job but also start working your business doing the exact same thing that you'll be doing if you're working your W-2 job. Because you have all the training and you know it. The only thing that's stopping you is "you".

Tell your Soon to be ex-wife or soon to be ex-husband that you and a family member or family friend are going in on the business together. Your family member or your friend is putting up most of the money to start the business but they're going to pay you just as soon as the business starts to take off. But for now they're just giving me 10% and giving me a 1099. But they still need my help. So, when I go to work I'll be at work on my W2 job. But when I get off from my 9:00 to 5:00 w-2 job. I'll be going to help my family members or best friends work the business that they started. This is going to kill two birds with one stone. You're soon to be ex-wife or ex-husband we'll think that you are actually doing what you say you're doing. Your soon to be ex-wife or soon to be ex-husband just don't know what's coming down the pipe for your soon to be ex-husband or soon to be ex-wife. The other thing that this accomplishes is that you are growing your business. I mean growing the person who you trust or your best friend's business now.

You're still playing it cool to your soon to be ex-husband or soon to be ex-wife. This also helps you stay away from your soon to be ex-husband or soon to be x-wife and gives you something to do. Have you ever been driving home down the street and you see that light on in the house and you know he or she is awake, those kids are still up and you just keep driving by like you don't live there. Working will give you something to do. So, all you have to do is go home, lay down and start all over again in the morning.

Say that you're working late. But actually, give your location. And you must, must, must not be talking to other women or men during this transition period. You must be very honest open and transparent to your soon to be ex-husband or soon to be ex-wife. They will get upset that you're working late, so share your location, let them see your phone, let them have your passcode to your phone, to disarm their trust. Don't have a second phone. And if you have a second phone for work… be honest open and transparent with that phone too. Anyone can pick up on the fact that you're not interested anymore. Again, please listen.

Anyone can pick up on the fact that you're not interested anymore. So don't even tempt yourself. This is part of the **Escape Plan**. If you have a valid excuse for coming home, working late and just want to go to sleep, that is understandable by any means. By you working late is bettering yourself for the future.

Don't even have the distraction. Don't even have the distraction. Don't even have the distraction of other men or women during this process.

Remember karma will come back for you. Your still married or in a relationship. Plant a good seed. Do good and help others, it shall be returned. If you plant a bad seed, do bad and destroy others, it shall be returned. Just as in equal amounts. For that, is the law of karma.

Grow your business while you're working your W-2 job, when your business is making just as much, if not more then your W-2 job. And you think you're ready to pull the trigger. Don't…

Start reading the newspaper. Yes, yes, my honeydew said it start reading a newspaper. It may seem stupid now, but it will make sense later on.

Keep a newspaper under your arm wherever you go. Make sure everybody sees it. Especially your soon to be ex-husband or ex-wife. Continue this, read an article or two but throw it away. Make sure your soon to be ex-husband or soon to be ex-wife sees you reading this newspaper consistently. Reading in bed at night before you go to sleep.

In Michigan it snows a lot through October all the way up until April. There's snow and ice everywhere. You must walk so carefully on the snow and ice as not too fall. But if you should so happen to find a patch of ice and fall or slip. Take a picture of yourself with your cell phone lying on the ground with the newspaper that has the present date on it. Hence getting punched in the face by a girl, and taking a picture with a newspaper the next morning, it was all the **Escape Plan**

Send that newspaper picture of you on the ground to your soon to be ex-husband or ex-wife. And tell them "I done slipped on this ice and hurt my back"… Who hasn't fallen on snow and ice in Michigan. Complain two your soon to be x husband or soon to be x-wife at your back hurts. Complain your back hurts when it's time to do the Lord's work….lol… funny. But being real, give off this illusion. And if you're ready to leave your soon to be ex. Sometimes you don't want them to touch you at all. You don't even feel like being around that person but continue to keep doing what you do. You know your not hurt. But sell it. And sell it good.

At your next annual checkup let the doctor know of your fall, have the picture of the ice and the newspaper, cause we all need to go to the doctor once a year and get your checkup. Men and women go get your checkup. Your health is your wealth. Let your doctor know that you fell on ice and snow and you just want to check your back because you've been having back pain. Now most jobs involve bending over, heavy lifting, standing up and walking. Some jobs involve sitting. Purchase a back lumbar support.. save the receipt. Save the paperwork that you stated to your doctor that you have back pain sometimes. Start going to physical therapy for your back pain. Save the receipts. Grow your business. Continue to go to physical therapy. It doesn't have to be every day but just make sure it's documented.

Then when you're ready to file for divorce or ready to move out of the home from your child's mother or father, do not.

Because now the person who you trust or your best friends business now owns a house, condo and a vehicle that is used as a home office and a vehicle that is used as a company vehicle.

Just know in your head that you're ready to file for divorce or move out.. But just know you must play the role for about two and a half to three years. Because honeydew knows that friend of the court will only go back the last two to three years to look at your income. And they will base your child support and alimony off your last two to three years of income. Do not give your soon to be ex a hard time, you will blow up your plan and spot, play it cool.

Sometimes you don't feel like going to work so don't because of your back pain. Your W-2 job will either have to terminate you or let you go because of your attendance. But you have chronic back pain that prevents you from sitting at a desk all day cuz you have to get up stand and stretch and walk where you work a job or you have to stand stretch and walk and carry heavy loads that will hurt your back. Now that your W2 job has let you go, you're only getting the 10% from your best friends business or the person you trust business.

Here comes the hard part..

Now you have to be willing to take a "L" for the next couple years to show that your income has been reduced because you have severe back pain. Survive below your means, sell it, sell it good. Stay behind the scenes. But know that in the back of your head that, you are securing your future. You are winning!

Not sure if you know, but strains to the muscles or tendons or ligaments that are in your back lack physical proof. You can get CT scans all day. But if you have pain in your back muscles. It's irrefutable evidence off of your verbal complaints of pain, that you have back pain which prevents you from doing your job. So now you just work every now and again with your best friend or the person you trust business and get paid the 10% that you guys or ladies signed a management contract for years ago..

Now when you're ready to file for divorce from your soon to be ex-wife or ex-husband you have almost a documented history of about 3 years where you have just made 10% on a 1099, that you work as a contractor for your best friends or somebody who you trust business. And that is only income that you've made for the last 3 years. You were let go from your W2 job or 1099 job for medical reasons and did not up an quit. But in your mind, know you have an **Escape Plan**.

That's the hard part. You have to be willing to take a loss for a while just to put yourself in a better position for after your divorce. What you must know is that every two years after you divorce and if you have to pay child support then Friend of the Court is going to automatically assess your income to see if you're making the same amount or more. But that good best friend that you have or that person that you trust knows your situation and they just want the best for you.

So now you need to have your best friend or the person you trust meet with an attorney and have them sign a trust. It needs to be stated that if something happens to your best friend or the person that you trust they have entrusted you and you have just inherited a business. Because it's inherited and it was left to you in a trust. Child support nor alimony cannot touch that. Your ex could try but they won't succeed. So now its time to ball out of control…

Honeydew tried breakin it down in the simplest form for me. But I think I understood what he was saying and he had all the paperwork to prove it. Honeydew is living proof. Sometimes you have to stay behind the scenes but know and be humble enough to know what you have inherited.

You have to be smart enough to understand you cannot let your past affect your future, so what you have to do is protect your future. Just because you file for divorce or leave your childs mother or father. That doesn't mean that your life has to go down the tank. But the system is designed that way.

Honeydew told me about this and if he didn't do these things way before he thought about filing for divorce he would be crying the Blues.

That's why he let me know up front, that he wasn't afraid to get married again. He just needs to have the person who he gets married to except that the only way he's going to get married is to sign a prenuptial agreement and a postnuptial agreement. Because he's been through the shit…

Not only does it protect him but it also protects me. And since I have worked hard to get to where I'm at as a nurse practitioner. You don't want somebody to rush into marriage with you and then decide, it just isn't working anymore, take half of everything. You have worked hard and your family worked hard for what you inherited. That other person did not take all those college courses. That other person did not have to stay up night, night after night studying. That other person did not have to sacrifice their life just to take a timed test or fix sewing machines.

That's why you need to let the person know that you wanna spend the rest of your life with, they must sign a prenuptial agreement and a postnuptial agreement. And if they don't, then that person has just showed you who they are up front.

And if they take a little time to come around to be ok with signing a prenuptial agreement and a postnuptial agreement, it's ok. Most people haven't even heard of a prenuptial agreement or postnuptial agreement. All they could think of is the bad about it. Be honest with them, share your knowledge with them of what you know about a prenuptial agreement and a postnuptial agreement. But what it really does is expose real love or fake love. And if they're not cool with signing a prenuptial agreement or a postnuptial agreement walk away.

But just ask them. Why do we even have to get married at all. Let's just be friends still hang out do what we do and the Lords work. But if they are dead set on getting married. Then you should be dead set on walking away. And if they're dead set on walking away after you told them that you don't need to get married just to be friends. That's like a flashing red light before You get hit by a train. Red flag.

Chapter 5

Proof the Escape plan Works

(The Cheater, The User, Cold Hearted Snake, Blindsider)

Lady E has a friend who does hair. She wants to be called "Juicenda to the stage"… Thank you, for letting us use your true story. She's been doing lady E hair forever. Lady E friend who does hair told lady E that she got married to her husband when lady E was first getting her hair done in her basement. Lady E friend bought a house on a main street, turned it into a hair salon. Lady E hair stylist friend, family, knew a guy that was good with running electric wiring, but under the table. Lady E friend and the guy who knew how to run electric wiring , and wired up her first house, to state code, on the main street that is now a salon, hit it off, got married and had two boys. They didn't get a pre-nup or post-nup. Lady E friend who does hair was able to buy a nice house in the suburbs of metro Detroit. Because she worked so much at her salon in Detroit, lady E friend bought another building closer to her home in the suburbs, so she could work closer to home. So now lady E's friend had a salon in Detroit and a salon in the suburbs.

Lady E's friend had beauticians and barbers that rented booths and kept her salon pumpin and jumpin, which gave her more time to be at home with her two boys and husband. With lady E's friend having more time at home she discovered that her husband *(The Cheater)* , is cheating. When lady E friend hair stylist contacted attorneys to file for divorce the attorneys let her know that her husband who did side work of electricity and got paid under the table would be able to take half of her hair salons and Lady E's friend would have to pay her husband's child support and alimony. Lady E knew of her situation way before she met honeydew. Lady E told her hair stylist friend of honeydews **Escape Plan**. Lady E hairstylist friend encouraged her husband to go back to school and become a master electrician and paid for his schooling. She also helped him start his own business and bought his first company van. Now when clients come into both of her salons and ask who did the electrical work. Lady E hairstylist friend refers them to her soon to be ex-husband. So now when lady E hairstylist friend wants to make a smooth getaway, her husband's electrical business that she helped him start all while knowing it was just the **Escape Plan** so she could keep her business, house and cars, now can file for divorce and keep her businesses while her ex-husband is gainfully employed as a master electrician and his own business that is documented with taxes. Lady E hairstylist friend is still waiting to pull the trigger. Because she doesn't wanna mess up the family dynamic with her 2 beautiful boys and father. Lady E hair stylist friend helped her soon to be ex-husband who she knows is still cheating, stay calm, cool and invest in her soon to be ex-husband. When lady E hairstylist friend is ready to file for divorce she will not lose her hair salon businesses to her ex-husband. Lady E hair stylist friend knows that her soon to be ex-husband's electrician business is her bargaining chip. Because lady E hair stylist friend contribute it to prosperity of her soon to be ex-husband, She will prosper in return. By keeping what she built from doing hair.

Honeydew told me of a childhood friend who got married without a prenuptial agreement and post nuptial agreement. *He wants to be called " Smart MF" ...* Thank you, for letting us use your true story. Him and his wife *(The User)* lived in an apartment. His father left him a house which was a lot bigger than the apartment that him and his wife were staying in at the current time.

Honeydew childhood friend was left the house because his father was getting up in age. Couldn't maintain the keep up of his big house and wanted to downsize.

His father, too, had filed for divorce long ago. A matter of fact his father gave Honeydew some of the best advice that honeydew said. Honeydew told his childhood friend Father that his second ex-wife and him were going through a hard time in his marriage. His second ex-wife was threatening him. Not only threatening him but hitting on him. One of the threats that his second ex-wife used to say now, that she had a better job which put her around people that make more money. His second x-wife used to state when she would get upset…. I'm going to divorce you. And I know men who make in the Millions.

And they holler at me all the time, but I have to shoot them down because I'm married to you, so just know that I could divorce you anytime and get with somebody who can be a better husband and a better father to our kids..

Honeydew told this to his childhood friend Father. Because he went into his childhood friend's father small business and saw him and he asked how things have been going. Honeydew said that his childhood friend's father had went through the ringer with his ex-wife and he had to file for divorce and ended up on the winning side because he was in a partnership with his business partner…. he co-owned the store currently that honeydew was at buying supplies and material. And he was one of the co-owners.

Honeydews childhood friends father told him, I'm sorry you going through that young man. But it reminds me of some of the stuff that my ex-wife used to say to me. But what I told her is. Yeah I'm probably sure these guys who make a whole lot more money than me…. probably could be a better father to our children and probably could give you a better life. But understand…. if you find that man attractive… don't you think another woman has found him attractive as well before you.. Don't you think another woman already has her claws in him because she knows the amount of money that he makes and how good of a guy he is.

So if you want to end our marriage…I'm fine with that. But just understand this mythological or fictional or real guy that you talking about….another woman already has their claws in him. So get ready to compete.

Shortly thereafter honeydew childhood friends father filed for divorce. He was awarded the house and able to keep the business that he co-founded.. He was able to file divorce and keep his life moving and not miss a Beat.. honeydew childhood friend Father even showed him pictures of him traveling now with his new female friends. Honeydews childhood friend's father said that the only way he would get married again is if a woman would agree to sign a prenuptial agreement and a postnuptial agreement protecting the business that he co-founded and any other thing that he was going to do in the future after they get married. But so far, he hasn't met anybody. He was an older gentleman but still running his small business, smiling laughing and joking and drinking coffee and greeting customers as they came in to his business.

This was Honeydew childhood friend, they grew up together, his house was right down the street from where he grew up. A nice big house. Right down the street from honeydew's family inherited house.

Well his childhood friend wife surprised him, and ended up filing for divorce. They didn't have a prenup. So, when she filed for divorce, she wanted to stay in honeydews childhood friends house. At the end of the divorce honeydews childhood friends credit, was not good enough to buy her out of the house.

Honeydews childhood friend x-wife legally evicted him out of his own childhood house. And didn't have to give him a penny... she legally evicted him out of his own childhood home, that he had grew up in and inherited. You have to say that twice. And honeydew childhood friend had to pay high child support when he was surprised with divorce papers because he had a W2 high paying job.

Honeydew childhood friend cried the blues. Now honeydew's childhood friend ex-wife lives in honeydew's childhood friends house for half of the price of what the house is for. And to add insult to injury. Honeydews childhood friend did not get a penny for the house. Honeydew's childhood friend had a 401k. Instead of Honeydew childhood friend having to split half of his 401k with his ex-wife that he paid into during the duration of their marriage. Which now she legally can take half of. he said and they agreed to her not taking half of his 401k but using half of his 401k to buy him out of his own childhood house that he inherited..

She never gave him a penny, she just agreed not to take half of his assets in exchange for his childhood house when his x wife filed for divorce.. Honeydew childhood friend ex-wife does hair and has two children. Honeydew childhood friend works at a major company in Michigan and has a college degree in computers. Honeydew's childhood friend ex-wife makes 1/4 of what honeydew's childhood friend makes on his W2 job. Now tell me that ain't gangster.

Now when honeydew goes to his childhood friends father's business to buy supplies. His childhood friends father says, I told that boy that that girl was no good. And look at what she did to him. Now honeydew childhood friend is living back in a apartment again, but now paying high child support because he can't just quit his W-2 job..

Back in the day when honeydew hung out with his childhood friend he would sing the blues about the bad decisions that he made. But also congratulates honeydew for being able to make a smooth getaway. And pay less child support than what he has to pay. Honeydew childhood friend also met another young lady.. They had a baby. But he doesn't want to get married again. Honeydews childhood friend asked honeydew for some advice what would he do if he was in his situation, if he must make a smooth getaway..

Honeydew asked his childhood friend do you want to get married again? He said no. Because she's already showing signs of what my ex-wife used to do. But I want to make a smooth getaway just like you did and not have to pay a lot of child support. Honeydew told him that he needs to invest in a business that he does now, that he gets his current W-2 employment. So, honeydews childhood friend, currently works for a major company. He got his degree in computers. He works with one of these major companies to develop cameras in vehicles. So my honeydew told his friend back in the day to invest in what you love to do…. If you invest in what you love to do…you can do this and not get paid but still have the thrill of doing what you love to do because you love it. So honeydew's childhood friend took his advice.

Honeydew also told his childhood friend that since you had a new child and you guys were not married.. Have your new child's mother file for child support…. Friend of the court can only take a percentage of your W-2 paycheck. Just because you have more children doesn't mean that you pay more. The percentage that friend of the court can legally take has to be split among all of your biological children. That would mean that the new child that you just had is going to take a percentage away from the child support that you already pay for your children to your ex-wife. Use that money to invest in yourself.

Honeydew told me that he ran back into his childhood friend and he told him that he started his own business buying high price drone cameras. And he bought a whole bunch of drone cameras and rents them out to people who want to shoot videos and use drones. He's also collaborating with another childhood friend of honeydews. And they're running a business together. Honeydew also said that his friend did put himself on child support for his new child. His child support never went up. They just deducted a percentage from the child support that he already pays his ex-wife and now it goes into the bank account of his current child's mother. Which she gives the money back to him. Honeydews child's friend states that he uses that money to pay for the apartment that him and his current child mother lives at. So even though child support is taken out of his W-2 check from one of the major companies here in Michigan. A percentage of that now goes to his current mother of his child which she in turn gives to him and they use that money to pay the rent. The money now that he is saving he has invested it into buying high price drone cameras and renting out.

Honeydew childhood friend understands that he has to protect his future. He's going to have to pay child support anyways cuz he's making these babies. So he just has to man up and do what he needs to do.

But honeydew childhood friend understands that he has a W-2 job. With the major company here in Michigan. He knows that his job has a lot of potential. And if he started his own business doing the exact same thing that he does for his W-2 job that he can make money off of it.

Honeydew's childhood friend loves computers technology and cameras. Honeydews childhood friend collaborated with another one of honeydew's childhood friends. Who is in a better situation than honeydew's childhood friend. They have collaborated together. He does the work and his friend takes the credit. So now if and when honeydew childhood friend decides to make the move, and pull the trigger. His business is already up and flourishing. Which is buying high price drones and renting them out to people who want to use them to make videos. Or using these high-priced drones with high price cameras to record videos for people, that they couldn't afford by themselves or could afford to buy but only want to use them for a short period of time.

Now that's honeydew's childhood friends business is starting to make more money than what honeydew childhood friend actually makes at his nine to five W-2 job. They just got contracted to make videos, using drones for a new project that is making stupid bread. Look at God,,,,,,,,,,,,,,,,,,,,,wont he do it.

Now, smart MF carries a newspaper, all he has to do is pull the trigger and sit down for a couple years. Collect his 10%. Allow 2 to 3 years to go by, wait for the big company to let him go because he has back pain and cannot walk for long periods of time or cannot stay seated for long periods of time because of his back.

Wait for his high price w-2 job to let him go because of his attendance for medical reasons. Let his child support get lowered…. And collaborate with his friend to still rent drones... Use that income that he rents drones with and purchase or rent a home office.

Pull his massive 401K, take a hit, before he gets let go from his W-2 job.

And work the business that he and his friend grew and get paid 10% from doing that. Now he just lowered his child support and his ex-wife who's living in the childhood home that he grew up in no longer is receiving a large child support payment because he had another child.

The **Escape plan** will lower the amount of money that his ex-wife and new childs mother was getting for child support. Because child support can only take a percentage out of your W-2 check or a percentage of your 1099. Your 1099 income can fluctuate so keep it at 10%. Now child support is coming in for the other child that he made. And now he is living off of a 10% business that honeydews childhood friends created.

So in about 2 to 3 years when child support sees that he has lost his job he has the documentation to show that he can no longer sit for long periods of time and he can no longer stand because of long periods of time because of his chronic back pain. They will be forced to let him go. Now he can make a smooth getaway from his child's mother who he just had the newborn with he can also make a smooth getaway from his ex-wife who legally took his childhood family home. Still make 10% of a business that his friend owns. And keep everything moving and he's making more than what he would have made if he was at his W-2 job. It's just that simple.

Honey dew's other childhood friend. He wants to be called Harley queef, l,m,a,o,… shout out to you and thanks for being down wit it.. …letting me use your story……. You hood rat… When he saw that honeydew was going through his divorce with his second ex-wife. Honeydew childhood friend knew about honeydew plan from origination and watching it unfold in real life.

Honeydew's childhood friend let him know that his wife *(Cold Hearted Snake)*, was exemplifying and doing things that she know if he did…. she would be pisssed off. She was hanging out on the weekends, not coming home. Also leaving him with the children and hanging out. Saying that she was at a relative's house helping them on the weekdays and weekends because they were older in age.

Honeydew told his childhood friend that she's about to get ready to file for divorce. Honeydew saw the red flags way before it happened. Just pay attention to the Red Flags. Honeydew's childhood friend said, Nah….she'll never do that….we solid… She's just really helping out a relative. Honeydew said, yeah OK, that's BS and sugar honey ice tea, believe what you want. But trust me you need to pull your 401K, which is very large.

Honeydew divorce from his second ex-wife finally wrapped up. And honeydew was able to make a clean smooth getaway. When honeydew's childhood friend saw this…..he asked, what honeydew would do…if he was in his situation.

Honeydew childhood friend has a job that give tons of overtime. Honeydew's childhood friend works a lot of volunteered overtime. Honeydew told his childhood friend, pull your massive 401K which you have deposited money in to since 1996. You're going to have to take a hit, by a government agency with three letters or your soon to be ex-wife. Which one will hurt more? Giving up 33% which your gonna have to do anyways…. Or 50% plus 33% of your 401k that you stacked bank in.

Trust and believe your soon to be ex-wife is about to file for divorce. Stop working overtime now. So, honeydew's childhood friend pulled his massive high six figure 401K. Without telling his soon to be ex-wife and slowed down working overtime to be more involved in his children's life.

And just as the sky is blue and the day is long. Honeydew's childhood friend was sitting at home with his boys. And he heard a knock at the door. It was a process server. He just got served, with divorce papers. Real talk. Honeydew's childhood friend immediately called honeydew. Honeydew's childhood friend said, "I can't thank you enough". My wife just filed for divorce… Honeydew wished his childhood friend Condolences on his loss. They both laughed….Honeydew asked, could you please read me what is on the complaint for divorce. Honeydew childhood friend ex-wife was asking for full custody of their children and half of his 401K.

Honeydew friend came over to his house. I was there. They laughed and laughed and laughed and laughed.

So when honeydew's childhood friend had to fill out affidavits stating his assets. When it came down to his use to be large 401K. He put $10 and also had the documentation to prove it. So when honeydew's childhood friend ex-wife went to court with her male attorney who thought he was going to get paid, because honeydews childhood friend x-wife male attorney knew that honeydew's childhood friend had a massive 401K. He quickly picked up the case. But to honeydew's childhood friend x-wife and her male attorneys surprise.

Honeydew childhood friend 401K was completely empty. And because honeydew's childhood friend pulled his money before he got served with divorce papers. How could he ever know that he was going to go through a divorce.

What he did with his money… who knows…. but once it's gone, it's gone. And if it was pulled before served with divorce papers. You have legal Plausible deniability now. Honeydews childhood friend did not know that his now ex-wife was going to serve him with divorce papers. He was trying to be the best husband that he could be. Honeydew's childhood friend ex-wife got dropped by her male attorney and had to go to mediation because she couldn't afford an attorney and ended up getting less child support and no alimony.

Now Honeydew's childhood friend is not working overtime. Which now lowers his W2 income. Which now lowers his child support.

But ask yourself this question, why does he have to work overtime if he's already sitting pretty, divorced and single….ready to mingle, has alot of change to spend, if he want to feel a tingle.

Now tell me that ain't gangster.

The students who have been taught hard lessons are sharing knowledge and now becoming masters.

So when I told honeydew that I have written a book for him and his friends success stories, I put one of his childhood friends success story in the book. Honeydew just laughed and laughed and laughed. He said how did you know all this. Lady E said I know you did all this because I hang out with you and all your childhood friends. And you guys laugh and laugh and laugh about your stories. And I see how thankful they are to you, when you guys laugh and joke. And even sometimes cry laughing. But you could tell that they're really happy. And then some of your friends who you didn't tell your **Escape Plan** too, how they don't have that same laugh or don't even laugh at all. They cry the blues, they legit cry the blues, you can see it in their body language, their not happy and settling.

So, honeydew said, I love you and thank you for writing me this book. But I have to ask my childhood friends if it's okay for me to put their story out there as well as mine. I said yeah sure. So when honeydew told his childhood friends. They laughed as well. They laugh laugh laugh. They only have one stipulation. Don't use my name. Which honeydew didn't.

But honeydew had one childhood friend who had one demand. He didn't want his name to be put out there. Which honeydew and Lady E, totally understood. But instead of being called honeydew childhood friend he wanted to be called a certain name. Honeydew and his childhood friend laughed and laughed and laughed and laughed. Honeydew said, okay because his true story was just absolutely bananas..

So this is honeydew talking not Lady E. So, my childhood friend said that he wanted his name to be a certain name. I said, man, ain't no way in hell, another grown man is going to call you that. And we laughed and laughed. But his story. You just have to hear.

So this is a shout out from honeydew to my childhood friend who wanted to be called "cucumber pickle". LMAO. You only get one shout out like that, you hood rat.

Back to Lady E

So honeydews childhood friend story was the most diabolical. His story happened a long time ago. But he started using the **Escape Plan** several years ago.

He was married and one day his ex-wife *(The Blindsider)* , gave him divorce papers. And she moved out the house before the lease ended. So honeydew's childhood friend stayed at the house and renewed the lease in his name only. While honeydew childhood friend was at his house he received some mail.

It was friend of the court paperwork saying that he was in the arrears to the tune of about $25,000. So he called Friend of the Court and said she just gave me divorce paperwork how can I be in the arrears of $25,000. Friend of the court told him that his ex-wife came down to the court a couple years ago. And said that you had moved out of the house and stated that you were going to file for divorce. So, Friend of the Court put him on child support.

His ex-wife told Friend of the Court that she didn't know where he was at, the only address she had for him was the address that he was currently living at.

Now honeydews childhood friend had lived at that house every single day and had never left. But his ex-wife lived at the house as well. Honeydews childhood friend had a job that made very good money but require him to work a minimum of 8 hours a day. But if you want it overtime, he could be able to work 12 hours a day or even 16 hours a day. Honeydew childhood friend job that he worked was carpentry. So when overtime was available he took it. That kept him out of the house a lot. But he was working. To pay all of the bills at the house. So with him not being at the house when mail got delivered his ex-wife would take the mail and only give him certain pieces of mail. The pieces of mail she did not give him was the child support friend of the court paperwork.

Honeydews childhood friend called Friend of the Court when he received that mail. I have all of the receipts from where I paid the lease at this house and how could I be $25,000 in the arrears. They advise honeydews childhood friend to hire an attorney and make a court date. But honeydews childhood friend already had an attorney because of the divorce. He asked the attorney to add this in to divorce case. His attorney said yes but said that would be another retainer. Because it was a different matter. Honeydew's childhood friend did have the money to pay for his divorce, but not also pay to fight this $25,000 arrears from Child support. So honeydew friend just paid for his divorce. After honeydews friend divorce was final which didn't take long. Honeydew's childhood friend up, and quit his job. Because he said he wasn't going to pay all that money for child support.

Honeydew's childhood friend ex-wife pretty much made the same amount of money. When she filed for divorce, she was not able to get alimony. But she was awarded full custody of the children and would not let him see his children. His attorney said that he could fight to get joint custody but that will be another retainer fee that he would have to pay.

Honeydew childhood friend did not have the money to pay the retainer because paying for an attorney for his divorce wiped him out.

Honeydew's childhood friend, up, and moved to the Southern States. Honeydew's childhood friends started doing the Lord's work in southern states, Midwest states and eastern states. Spreading seeds ever where... So much to the tune of him having six baby mamas, and six figure child support arrears. Honeydew childhood friend accrued large amounts of Friend of the Court expenses in several states.

It wasn't until honeydew childhood friend was driving and he was pulled over. Not because he had bad plates on his car, not because he had no insurance. He was pulled over because when the officer ran honeydew's childhood friend name. He had unpaid child support. Because he had unpaid child support Friend of the Court suspended his license. He was issued a ticket his car was towed and impounded and advised to take care of his child support debt.

So honeydew childhood friend said he would leave the country. work in carpentry and was good with his hands... Lol.... Friend of the court thought of that too. So he went to try to apply for a passport. He received a denial notice saying that he cannot leave the country because of his unpaid child support.

So honeydew's friend asked him if he could get help to pay his child support so he can get his license back active. Honeydew did help. Honeydew also told him that this is what he must do so that way he can get his license back and also pay little on his child support.

Honeydew childhood friend worked in carpentry. Honeydew childhood friend collaborated with someone he trust. The person who he trusted started a business in carpentry. Honeydews childhood friend went out and did the work. Honeydew childhood friend signed a management contract with the person he trusted. The person who he trusted, issued him a 1099 only making 10% of what the person who he trusts business was bringing in.

Honeydew childhood friend did this for about two and a half years. Honeydew's childhood friend filed timely taxes on those two years of 10% income . With help from honeydew, his childhood friend and honeydew made a fellas trip out of it, partying out of control. They went to all of the states that Honeydews childhood friend, Friend of the Court cases were in, hung out and partied. They took ride share, to Friend of the Court, lit and laughing, in all those States and filed paperwork asking for modification on honeydew's childhood friends child support.

They gave Friend of the Court his two years of taxes. They gave friend of a court of valid address that honeydew's childhood friend could be reached at. Honeydew and his childhood friend came back home. Honeydew's childhood friend then received paperwork on the modification of his child support. Lowering his child support down.

Now honeydews childhood friend still has arrears. But he was able to get his license back active. Get on payment plan. Honeydew's childhood friend does still have to pay child support, but it's for a much lower amount. Unfortunately, he still cannot get a passport, until he owes less than $2,500 in child support, to spread more seed out the country…. Lmao. But he's able to drive clean now and not have to worry.

Honeydew childhood friends story took the cake. That's why I, Lady E, had to write honeydew story. His childhood friends' stories, well, they just have to be shared. Currently honeydew and his childhood friends get together out on the water and they laugh laugh laugh laugh. I know because I'm there laughing with them.

Some of honeydew's friends took large hits. Some of Honeydews friends made a smooth getaway like him. Some of honeydews friends hang out on the water and cry the blues. But honeydew childhood friends who he told his **Escape**

Plan, are living successful happy lives, Not crying the Blues and paying little child support.

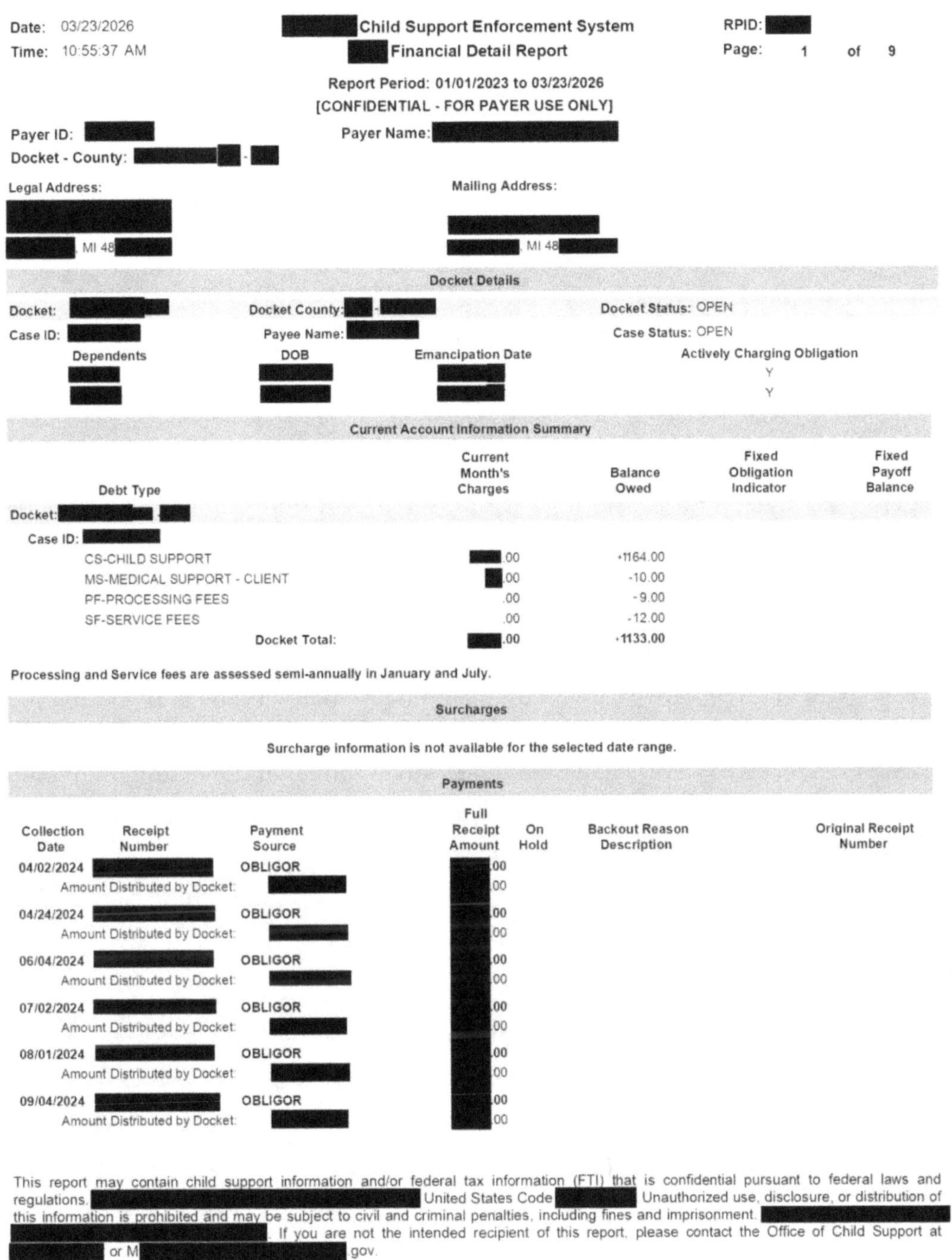

Date: 03/23/2026   ▮ **Child Support Enforcement System**   RPID: ▮

Time: 10:55:37 AM   ▮ **Financial Detail Report**   Page: 1 of 9

Report Period: 01/01/2023 to 03/23/2026

[CONFIDENTIAL - FOR PAYER USE ONLY]

Payer ID: ▮   Payer Name: ▮

Docket - County: ▮ - ▮

Legal Address: ▮ , MI 48▮

Mailing Address: ▮ , MI 48▮

Docket Details

Docket: ▮   Docket County: ▮ - ▮   Docket Status: OPEN

Case ID: ▮   Payee Name: ▮   Case Status: OPEN

Dependents	DOB	Emancipation Date	Actively Charging Obligation
▮	▮	▮	Y
▮	▮	▮	Y

Current Account Information Summary

Debt Type	Current Month's Charges	Balance Owed	Fixed Obligation Indicator	Fixed Payoff Balance
Docket: ▮				
Case ID: ▮				
CS-CHILD SUPPORT	▮.00	+1164.00		
MS-MEDICAL SUPPORT - CLIENT	▮.00	-10.00		
PF-PROCESSING FEES	.00	-9.00		
SF-SERVICE FEES	.00	-12.00		
Docket Total:	▮.00	+1133.00		

Processing and Service fees are assessed semi-annually in January and July.

Surcharges

Surcharge information is not available for the selected date range.

Payments

Collection Date	Receipt Number	Payment Source	Full Receipt Amount	On Hold	Backout Reason Description	Original Receipt Number
04/02/2024	▮	OBLIGOR	▮.00			
Amount Distributed by Docket:		▮	.00			
04/24/2024	▮	OBLIGOR	▮.00			
Amount Distributed by Docket:		▮	.00			
06/04/2024	▮	OBLIGOR	▮.00			
Amount Distributed by Docket:		▮	.00			
07/02/2024	▮	OBLIGOR	▮.00			
Amount Distributed by Docket:		▮	.00			
08/01/2024	▮	OBLIGOR	▮.00			
Amount Distributed by Docket:		▮	.00			
09/04/2024	▮	OBLIGOR	▮.00			
Amount Distributed by Docket:		▮	.00			

Chapter 6

Red Flags To Look Out For and What To Expect

(Milk and Cookies)

Red flag to look for, if anyone puts hands on you. Leave immediately.

Red flags to look for, somebody who is constantly saying they're going to leave or divorce you. Don't talk about it. be about it. Let them leave and you be silent, watch them come running back.

Why don't you just do it, why don't you just leave, why don't you just get a divorce. But if they're constantly threatening you with divorce, 9 times out of 10 they don't mean it, they're just trying to get a reaction out of you. Don't react, they're just waiting to get a reaction out of you. Stay cool and calm. Understand, maybe you have done something wrong and they're speaking out of anger. And that person is just letting you know, you got one more time, then you're through. But if they continually say they're going to get a divorce or leave when you just being you. It's at that time that you must understand, that is a red flag.

Red flag to look out for...... People who out of no where get your name tattooed on them. Red Flag.... Tats are cool. Matching tattoos are even cooler. But when discussed and agreed upon. But if someone just pops up and says out of thin air ....Surprise!!!!!!!!! .... I got yo name tatted on me...... Red flag... then next question will be........ Do you like it?......... Can you get, my named......Tatted on you?........................ yeah ....Thats, a Hard, No..........Red Flag....

Red flag to look for, Someone who doesn't have time for you. Being around your child's mother or child's father or husband or a wife. People make time for what they want. And it is not up to you to tell the person that they need to spend time with you. It's up to that person to know that, they need to spend time with you.

But you must also, allow them grace for the person who you want to spend time with you. You must understand that, they have things that they need to do during the day that tires them out, they need time to decompress. And sometimes those things that they do can be very tiring. If that person is extremely tired, but still making time to be with you. You have to accept it for what it is. And if that person is extremely tired and falls asleep on you, but is still with you. You must know that they're trying their hardest after working a long day or being very busy. Just to spend time with you and you must give them grace.

But the difference is when they stop spending time with you. They could be extremely tired. But they could be somewhere else, and there not with you.

Red flag to look for, people who constantly throw up in your face about what other people could do for them. Then just let them do it. But sometimes you find out the grass is not greener on the other side. The grass is greener where you water it and fertilize it. And do you know what it takes to make beautiful green grass, water which is gonna feel like you're drowning, fertilizer which has a certain odor to it that a lot of people can't stand. But it makes for greener grass.

Red flag to look for, someone who is not giving you peace. Some people dwell in drama. They wake up in the morning and have to find something wrong. Their peace is creating drama for others. They always make stuff harder than what it has to be. If there's a simple problem, there is a simple solution. Don't overthink it, keep it simple smarty.(k.i.s.s). Don't be the person Keeping it Drama, (K.I.D)

Red flag to look for people who constantly complain about money. You have your health and time. Your health is your wealth. Your time is your most valuable asset. It's worth more than gold. When will that person realize, you're powerful beyond your imagination. Stop complaining about were your at in life. You're at, where your at, because of your past choices. Understand it and move on.

Either you're gonna have depression because you're sad about your past decisions.

Or You're gonna have anxiety about the future and what's ahead.

Don't stress over yesterday. You can't change the past. You must understand this, out of today is born tomorrow, just do your best today, give it your all, and watch it pay off tomorrow. It's not how much money you have, it's what you do with it. Everyone has 24 hours in a day, what you do with it is your choice. Why is it that some get more accomplished than others in 24 hours? Just run your race. But, just remember you only have one life to live. And that time clock is forever running until your batteries run out. Mother nature and father time are undefeated. Your going to get older. How you treat people now, is how people will treat you later, be nice, help everyone, give more of yourself. Make the most of those 24 hours. Divorce, baby mamas, baby daddies, layoffs, illnesses, shit happens. It's all a part of the process of life. Don't complain about it, do something about it. All it's gonna do is make you stronger if you just get back up or keep playing the game. Have patience, welcome your pain, embrace your pain, learn from your pain, smile at your pain, then be able to laugh at your old pain. Just have patience, take a knee, weather the storm you're in, rest up, know and trust, its going to work out. Your pain is just temporary. Cry it out to you can laugh it out. When is winning easy? Your pain will make you stronger... Brothers and Sistas, stay strong. Learn to be content in whatever situation you're in. Whether well fed or hungry, rich or poor. You can make a heaven out of hell or you can make a hell out of heaven. Men don't give up, neither do women. If you've been dealt a bad hand, play again change your cards or change your woman or man until you win. People will continue to break your heart until you find a nurse practitioner who could fix it.

Red flag to look for, travel. Spend a little money, to learn a lesson. Travel with somebody, do not spend a lot of money on this. It is just a test, that will save you money in the future. If it goes great, you'll have a good time. And you and that person will have memories of where you went for life, and travel more with that person. But, If it goes horrible, its what they call, "bought sense, you had to spend a lil money to learn a lesson", but lesson learned, now you will be smarter, moving forward in this relationship, if you want it to continue. Or now you know it wasn't meant to be. If that person complains about the flight, or hotel, or places that you're paying for them to go to. Red flag. Why are you complaining, if you haven't paid a dime toward this trip and you've never been out of the country once. Matter of fact, you don't even have your passport. Red flag.

If you make it to the point where you do want to travel with somebody. Travel out of the state 1st , don't spend a lot of money. Then 2nd , out of the country, this will be a great way to tell if you can get along.

Because once out of the state or out of the country. You and that person are now together, outside of both of your comfort zones, your hometown. It's a long way back to were ever yall from. So now you're forced to be together 24 hours a day, for a couple of days. Traveling with somebody on a crowded flight with seats by the bathroom to save money on flight and staying in a small hotel room really shows you the person that you're with, the good, the bad and the stinky. Lol..

Red flag to look for, someone who is not reciprocating. It is not your job to take care of somebody, they are a grown adult, not a child. If you do help somebody, they should be willing to help you with equal or greater amount of help. If you are not an asset to a person, you are a liability. You're an anchor, pulling that person down and keeping them stuck. A tiny anchor can hold down a very large ship.

Red flag to look for, words do not match the person's actions. If somebody is telling you what they're gonna do and doesn't do it in a timely fashion, their words do not match their action. It's simple, say what you mean, and mean what you say, then deliver. If you can't do something, just be humble enough to say it.

Red flag to look for, not wanting you to meet their closest friends or family.

Red flag to look for, not communicating about everything and I mean everything. Be honest, open and transparent, How can you coexist if you don't know what's going on. If you want to surprise somebody, then tell them that you want to surprise them or I could just tell you now but it will ruin the surprise. Be honest, give that person a chance to make the choice of if they wanna get surprised or wait. Then deliver the plan or make the surprise happen. Either or, they're gonna be surprised because what you're doing for them, they won't expect.

Red flag to look for, do not ever ever ever ever ever request for somebody to share their location with you Or phone lock code.. You're setting yourself up for failure and you will be very disappointed when you hear the word No.. Don't even put somebody in that position. But if that person should happen to volunteer to share their location or lock code, then allow them. They're just trying to be honest and that is a great quality. Do not go through their phone, show restraint, because you might go looking for something and you might find it or you might make something out of nothing and end up in a worse situation, the fact that they're allowing you to have their location and giving you their lock code shows trust. But if their phone breaks or they get another phone. Do not ever ever ever ever ever ask them why they haven't shared their location or lock code with you again. If they do not volunteer their location or lock code, that's a red flag. Or if their location link stops working. Politely let them know, 1 time, the lock code and location link don't work anymore. Please be polite. Watch your tone and your delivery. Ask very nicely, I cannot stress this enough. Do not dwell on it. You're setting yourself up for failure and disappointment. If they want you to have their new lock code or location they'll share it. If they do not investigate why their location isn't working or send another location link, red flag.

Red flag to look for, Respect, it's a very broad topic. But trust your gut. If somebody respects you enough, they're not gonna make a public fool of you. They're an adult, they know what they're doing. Anytime somebody disrespects you in private, public, social media or in front of friends, or family, not cool. The person that is your significant other should always take into account of how you will be affected by their actions. Your significant other should always want the best for you. Just think about it. Would they talk to their boss that way or would they act that way on their job? So, if they don't respect you, red flag.

Red flag to look for, People who don't want their x's to be happy. You should want your Ex to be happy. If your Ex is happy, they're leaving you alone, and moving on with their life, Co-parenting for the best interests of the child in common, great. That's not always the case. But if you get with someone who still wants bad for their, ex……… Red flag. Our Ex's are great people, with great stories, we're just meant for different books now. You should want good for your Ex. Again, if you're Ex's are happy, you will be happy, because they're leaving you alone and moved on,……………great. Honeydew said, he could tell when his ex-wives didn't have anybody, because they kept taking him back to court to try to get more money, lol.

But imagine when, you switch places, with the woman or man, who is your, Ex's baby Mama or ex-baby daddy. He or she will treat you the same way, that they are treating their current ex baby Mama or ex baby daddy. Recognize the Red flag.

When I met honeydew, he told me, what it was,…….. I told him, what it is. We knew we chose wrong, going forward in the future we may have issues with the people we had children with. Because we want the best for our children and the best is seeing our children happy. Lets just take one of our real life examples.

This example is called **(Milk and Cookies)**.. true story, real talk.

My last baby daddy signed my 10 year old daughter up for a girl's club. You are a great dad., Thanks. She has to sell cookies for the club she's in. So when she came to mom, Lady E and honeydew, and asked us to buy cookies, we did. Lady E and honeydews friends also bought cookies. What we didn't know is, that if Honeydew, and Lady E, friends didn't have the cookie shipped directly to them………Then the cookies will have to be delivered by daughter or parent who signed up the child. Cool, there's nothing wrong with that, in a rose colored world. Lady E's daughter cookie sales did great. Honeydews mice making sweater business and family inheritance made a large order. That set off a red flag. Someone, got upset about the large order that Honeydew made for Lady E, daughter. Lady E, nor, Honeydew knew this would happen. Honeydew was just trying to support. Lady E, called and asked the cookie company, if the orders of cookies, could be separated. No shade to the cookie company. The company was very helpful, apologetic and professional. But the orders were already placed and were being shipped. There was nothing they could do. They gave Lady E the proper forms to fill out to ensure this would never happen again, because they've never seen a situation like Lady E and

Honeydews, pissed off baby daddy drama over some milk and cookies… If we didn't receive the cookies from Lady E daughter within a week of delivery, call back in a week and they will start an investigation over cookies.Lol. Lady E and Honeydew just wanted to keep the peace, Honeydew was fine with taking a "L" on the cookies.

He's trying to get his six pack back, going to Costa Rica to cliff dive, and didn't need to be tempted by those scrumptious cookies, Lol. The rest of Lady E friends and family who ordered cookies, Lady E refunded them out of her own pocket.

Because Lady E, knew the drama, that was waiting ahead. And guess what, just as sure as the sky is blue and the day is long, when the cookies were delivered, my daughters baby daddy, only dropped off one box of $5 cookies. Out of all of Lady E and honeydew cookie orders totaling $1000. Lady E prepared for this and called her friends and honeydew's friends and let them know this before it happened.

When it was time for Lady E's friends to get their cookies that they had purchased. Lady E's baby daddy had already reached out to them over text, because he had Lady E and Honeydews friends numbers that were on their cookie order. Baby daddy advised their friends to come see him directly, if they wanted to pick up their milk and cookies, lol. But Lady E and Honeydew had already reached out to their friends and let them know the situation before the order arrived, and refunded them out of their own pockets. Lady E and Honeydews friends responded, keep the MF milk and cookies over text, so they wouldn't have to deal with the baby daddy drama, LOL. Because they already knew what time it was.

Lady E and Honeydew just wanted to keep the peace. Some people will continue to create drama, even over some milk and cookies….l,m,a,o… No matter what. If that is how they're treating their current baby mama or current baby daddy, just imagine how they would treat you when you switch places. Red flag, pay attention to the signs. Your baby daddy or baby mama should just want peace, not drama. Especially given their former situation and circumstances.

When you're ready to file for divorce from your soon-to-be ex-husband or soon to be ex-wife. Going the route of mediation will be the easiest and the cheapest way to do it. But one way you can tell if somebody is truly an honestly a toxic person. Is when you get ready to file for divorce or leave.

They should just understand that it doesn't work anymore. So instead of costing us both a lot of money hiring attorneys trying to figure this divorce out. Let's just hire a mediator. You say what you want to keep, I say what I want to keep, cuz I paid for it all, got the credit card receipts to prove it, and we make the split. Or just keep it all, I was tired, of that old shit anyways, I'll just buy everything new tomorrow. A toxic soon to be ex-husband or soon to be ex-wife, will prolong a divorce that could easily take 3-6 months....into several years. That's when you know you have a bitter toxic ex-husband or ex-wife. And that toxic ex-h usband or ex-wife has been that way since you met them from day one. Because they're back is against the wall, now they're really about to show you who they are. Trust, trust, trust, that Ex is going to come begging back... like clockwork.. you just have to be strong enough to know that, what's in front of you, is far, way much better than what's behind you.

Buckle up and get ready for the ride cuz it's about to be bumpy.

Start Living your Life

Its as easy as algebra math.

Simple, basic fundamental algebraic formula representing the sum of

two variables C = A + B

Success = Failures + One More Try

Success = Honeydew + Lady E

Keep Trying No Matter What

You bought this book, you just answered your own question. Now act!!!

A self-help book, written by a High Value Woman, for High Value Men, based off true stories of a High Value Man!

My name is "Lady E". I am a Nurse Practitioner A.G.A.C.N.P., my husband "Honeydew", What up doe, Detroit what it do. Honeydew, family owns successful businesses. Here is our true story…… all public information…and in our first amendment right as USA citizens for "freedom of speech"!!!

Most people say they want to start a business, so they look up business plans or take a class to start a business to be successful. If you want to eat an apple pie, buy a slice or take a baking class or just look up the recipe. Eat and smile. l. o. l.

Have you ever asked yourself the question, is my husband, wife, baby mommas, baby daddies or these children holding me back? How much further would I be in life, if they were out of my life? It's funny, yet so true. l. o. l. Men, women, children can be like anchors, pulling and holding you down if you choose wrong, so choose wisely. But what if you made the mistake and chose wrong. Maybe, you would be more successful in life without them dragging you down? Do you feel like you're drowning?

But you're worried about the consequences if you leave to breathe, how will leaving, affect your success afterward. Divorce & Attorneys are expensive, then thinking about child support and alimony you must pay afterwards, if you just drop the children off & leave, l. o. l. , makes people stay in horrible situations. Well, just like wanting to start a business, to be successful, you must make a business plan. My Honeydew had to create a business **Escape Plan** to leave his second ex-wife, to continue being successful.

Honeydew said, he learned a long time ago with his 1st divorce, playing by your Ex's, games, and the courts game, you will lose. But when you play, your own game, you have a much better chance of winning.

Honeydew, figured out how to lower his child support from $4200 a month, to $800 a month, Child Support refunding honeydew with an overage refund. (see Chapter 5, Your **Escape Plan** and picture of redacted child support refund credit). Now, when have you ever heard child support giving money back to the father. Honeydew pays no alimony, sees his children, if & when Honeydew wants, and continued to be successful. Honeydew & Lady E, want to save you, paying over six figures for attorneys, time, and stress. Buy the **Escape Plan** for the low low. Trust and believe, you will Thank us later.

Honeydew life lessons that he learned from his 1st divorce, made him come up with an **Escape Plan** for his 2nd divorce, with a pre-nup, when he recognized red flags that his second marriage was going down the toilet. Remember people are not afraid of lions roar. They're afraid of his bite. His **Escape Plan** protected his family inherited businesses; he didn't have to pay alimony and only very low child support, when he filed for divorce from his second marriage with children. He has also helped his other friends and LadyE friends. Now it's time for our story to help others!!!!! You too can lead a calm, peaceful, happy, joyous, prosperous life..

If you feel you chose wrong. Follow my Honeydew **Escape Plan!** This short-read book will teach you what red flags to pay attention to in your current relationship, how to make a smooth escape. Or if you're looking to be in a relationship with a high value woman or high value man, what red flags to pay attention to. What, to do, and what, not to do. So, you don't choose wrong, or don't get, chose at all!, There's P, in the pool, Its like, musical chairs out here in this dating world. Do you wanna be left standing up?

Everything that happened in this book is true. Business names, and persons names, have been changed in this book, to protect people's identity. You must fly under the radar when you're messing with somebody's money…. And fate.

You never know what people are going through. Alot of people are suffering in silence. Please share this book with all you know.. Don't boot leg it, l. o. l. Share the purchase link and encourage them to call National Domestic Violence Hotline 800-799-7233, and start your **Escape Plan**…..

Checkmate